INTRODUCTION

A
t the Nationalisation of Britain's railways in January 1948, the Scottish Region inherited over 1,400 locomotives which had been constructed by the pre-grouping companies, namely the Highland Railway (HR), Great North of Scotland Railway (GNoSR), North British Railway (NBR) and Caledonian Railway (CR). The largest numbers by far were of ex-CR and ex-NBR design with over 750 and 600 examples respectively. GNoSR survivors numbered just forty-three locomotives, while the HR was represented by only twenty-eight. Unfortunately, no engines from the Glasgow & South Western Railway survived to work with British Railways.

The GNoSR was by far the smallest in track mileage of the pre-grouping Scottish companies incorporated into the Scottish Region of British Railways, the bulk of it being single track with its locomotives being generally accepted as some of the most graceful looking to work on any railway in Britain. The 4–4–0 wheel arrangement dominated with thirty-nine examples of LNER D40 and D41 classes surviving to remain working with British Railways after Nationalisation. These could be seen working throughout the old GNoSR system and were based in sheds at Elgin, Keith, Inverurie and Kittybrewster where the crews and shed staff kept them in immaculate condition. All were withdrawn by June 1958 with the last example being retained by British Railways; former Class F (LNER Class D40) no. 62277 *Gordon Highlander* entered Inverurie Works and was completely repainted in an earlier GNoSR livery, given its original number 49, and subsequently utilised on special workings until finally being placed on static display in the Glasgow Museum of Transport during 1966.

With the withdrawal of many old and worn-out locomotives during the late 1920s, the GNoSR section of the LNER suffered a locomotive shortage that was rectified with the transfer of ex-GER Class S69 (LNER Class B12) 4–6–0s. Examples were allocated to Kittybrewster and Keith sheds from 1931 onwards, and by 1942 a total of twenty-five class members had migrated north. With a maximum axle loading of just over 15 tons these locomotives were ideal for working both passenger and goods traffic on the main line to Keith and Elgin, the Ballater branch and the Speyside line. They continued working in the area until being replaced by the Edward Thompson-designed Class B1 4–6–0s during the late 1940s and early 1950s, with the last of the Scottish Region allocated B12s being withdrawn during November 1954. In addition to the B12s, three ex-GER Class M15 (LNER Class F4) 2–4–2 tanks also found their way to the north-east of Scotland during 1931 and eventually were put to work on the St Combs branch. They were followed during 1948 by classmate no. 67157 which ended its days being well cared for as the Inverurie Works pilot before being withdrawn during June 1956 as the last example of the class.

The Highland Railway with its headquarters in Inverness ran through some of the most spectacular and severe railway operating country in Scotland with the climbs to County March on the far north line, Ravens Rock and Luib on the Kyle line, Dava on the original main line from Forres to Aviemore and the long drags of Slochd and Drumochter (Druimuachdar) on the main line to Perth. As a result the Highland built some of the most powerful locomotives in Britain; designed by David Jones and Peter Drummond there were such evocative names as the

'Skye Bogie', 'Loch' and 'Ben' classes. In September 1894 they introduced the first locomotive class in Britain with a 4–6–0 wheel arrangement – designed by David Jones these powerful locomotives were at ease with both passenger and goods traffic. Fortunately one example of the class was retained, no. 103, and she now resides in the Glasgow Museum of Transport. During the early years of the twentieth century, the railway introduced further designs of 4–6–0 locomotives with Peter Drummond's 'Castle' class being followed by the Christopher Cumming-designed 'Clan' class. By 1935 the LMS was beginning to allocate the new William Stanier-designed Class 5 4–6–0 – or the 'Black 5' – to Perth and Inverness sheds and these proved both hard-working and reliable on the Highland lines. They slowly replaced the ageing Highland-built locomotives that were scrapped or relegated to minor duties and by the time of Nationalisation, the rare survivors of these classes totalled only twenty-eight locomotives made up of one 4–4–0 'Loch', eleven 4–4–0 'Small Ben' engines, two 0–4–4 tanks, one 4–6–0 'Clan', six 4–6–0 'Clan Goods' and seven 0–6–0 'Barney' locomotives primarily allocated to sheds in the far north of Scotland. The last Highland Railway locomotive to be withdrawn was the diminutive 0–4–4 tank no. 55053 during January 1957.

The territory of the NBR encompassed both the rich agricultural areas of Fife, East Lothian and Berwickshire, the border counties and the highly productive coalfields in Fife and the Lothians which were crossed by the Waverley Route. The NBR also owned the West Highland Railway and its extension to Mallaig, and had running rights north of Montrose into Aberdeen. As a consequence the railway gave much attention to its stable of goods locomotives with the result that no less than 303 examples of three 0–6–0 tender classes – J35, J36 and J37 – were inherited by British Railways. So reliable were these that ten years after Nationalisation there were still over 250 of them working, with one class, the J37, still being complete-as-built with 104 members. As a comparison, ex-NBR passenger locomotives inherited by British Railways consisted of a mere seventy-nine engines of the 4–4–0 wheel arrangement, the impressive and powerful 'Atlantic' class having all been withdrawn during the 1930s.

By 1958 only thirty-two examples of two classes remained working – the J30 'Superheated Scotts' and J34 'Glens' – both designed by William Reid and both powerful and reliable classes that by 1960 had all gone to the scrapyard, except for no. 62469 *Glen Douglas*. This was retained for restoration and in August 1959 was turned out in NBR livery, given its original number (256) and subsequently used on many special trains before being placed in the Glasgow Transport Museum. In a similar move to the class B12 locomotives moving north to GNoSR territory, the LNER were transferring examples of the very able and reliable Class K2 2–6–0s into ex-NBR territory with six examples going north during 1924. These were followed over the next eight years or so by a further twenty members of the class. Initially allocated to Eastfield in Glasgow they were quickly found to be ideal for working on the West Highland line and its extension to Mallaig, and during 1933 and 1934 thirteen were given the names of lochs near this route. British Railways also acquired a total of seventy-four 0–6–0 tank locomotives of NBR origin of which the earliest class was introduced during 1900. By 1958 more than forty examples were still working in yards around Edinburgh and Glasgow but by the end of 1962 all had been withdrawn.

The only other ex-NBR locomotives to survive into preservation are a Cowlairs Works-built veteran of 1887 in the form of Class G (LNER Class Y9) 0–4–0 saddle tank no. 68095 which was bought privately after withdrawal during December 1962 – she can now be seen in the Scottish Railway Preservation Society Museum at Bo'ness. The second is ex-NBR Class C (LNER Class J36) 0–6–0 no. 65243 *Maude* which is currently to be seen at the National Railway Museum in York. It seems fitting, therefore, that the last two main line steam locomotives to be withdrawn from service in Scotland in June 1967 were constructed by the NBR in 1897 and 1900 respectively, as part of their Class C (LNER Class J36) introduced in 1888.

The Caledonian Railway was the great rival of the North British – so much so that they participated in the so-called 'Railway Races' to the north from London which were surrounded by great publicity, firstly during 1888 to Edinburgh and again after the opening of the Forth

Seen here at Kittybrewster shed in Aberdeen is one of the four diminutive Manning Wardle & Co. 0–4–2 tanks purchased by the GNoSR during 1915 for use on the harbour railways in Aberdeen. Still bearing its early LNER number, 6844 and wartime NE company identification, she would become no. 68191 with British Railways and be withdrawn from service during 1959. Compare this photograph taken in 1948 with that of the same locomotive in 1952 on page 35. *(K.H. Cockerill/ARPT)*

Railway Bridge during 1895 to Aberdeen. However, the serious and continuous rivalry was over goods traffic with the Caledonian heartland containing the heavy industries of steelmaking and ship-building in the Clyde valley and the huge Lanarkshire coalfield. Further afield the 'Caley' territory stretched as far north as Aberdeen, to Carlisle in the south and Oban in the west. This railway also gave great attention to its goods locomotive stock with a total of over 350 comprising five classes of 0–6–0 tender locomotives and 170 0–6–0 tanks coming into British Railways ownership. One class in particular, the 294 designed by Dugald Drummond and introduced during 1883, survived almost complete with over 150 examples all constructed during the nineteenth century coming into British Railway hands. The last examples of this class were not withdrawn until November 1963, having given almost eighty years of service. Caledonian-designed passenger locomotives surviving to become British Railways stock totalled less than 200, the bulk being the well-known 0–4–4 tanks, some dating from 1895 and others built by the LMS during 1925. These could be seen working branch lines all over the old Caley, Highland and GNoSR systems during the early 1950s and were still in use as occasional bankers on the climb to Beattock Summit. Surviving Caley-designed 4–4–0s and 4–6–0s were rarer with only three of the famous 'Dunalastair' 4–4–0 series and twenty-three Class 60 4–6–0s working into British Railways days. Miraculously all forty-eight examples of the William Pickersgill-designed successors to the 'Dunalastair' class engines were still working although allocated widely throughout Scotland. Examples could be seen working to Wick and Thurso, on the Highland main line between Perth and Inverness, and even to Kyle of Lochalsh. Further examples of the class were based at Greenock and at sheds throughout the old Glasgow & South Western Railway territory. Unfortunately all would be withdrawn by the end of 1962 and none of these beautifully proportioned locomotives survived into preservation. With the introduction of the 'Black 5' locomotives during 1934, the LMS were able to allocate increasing numbers of the class to ex-Caley sheds such as Polmadie and St Rollox in Glasgow, Dalry Road in Edinburgh and to Stirling and Oban. This allowed for the withdrawal of many older Caledonian locomotives with the remaining 4–6–0s all gone by the end of 1953. Three ex-CR locomotives did manage to survive into the preservation scene, the famous Caley single of the 1888 races, no. 123; Class 439 0–4–4 tank no. 55189, now to be seen at the Scottish Railway Preservation Society base at Bo'ness; and a Class 812 0–6–0 no. 57566 which is based with the Strathspey Railway at Aviemore.

Immediately after the Nationalisation of the railways in 1948, R.A. Riddles, who was responsible for mechanical and electrical engineering, set up a committee to make recommendations concerning the selection of the best existing locomotive types that would form the basis for a future construction programme. The main criteria for new locomotives were that they should be easy to service and repair, economical to work, offer improved driving and firing conditions for the crews, be cheap to build and have a wide route availability. The result was a list of twelve types ranging from a Class 7 Pacific to a Class 2 2–6–2 tank with provision later for a heavy goods locomotive. All twelve types were to be constructed with two cylinders, rocking grates and self-emptying ash pans.

The first of these new British Railways Standard locomotive types appeared in January 1951 when Pacific no. 70000 *Britannia* was rolled out of Crewe Works. The first of the Standards to be allocated to Scottish sheds during 1951 were five examples of the Class 5 4–6–0, nos 73005 to 73009, which were based at Perth. These were quickly followed early in 1952 by five 'Clan' 4–6–2s nos 72000 to 72004, allocated to Polmadie shed. The same year saw ten of the new Class 4MT 2–6–4 tanks being delivered to Polmadie, Corkerhill and Kittybrewster sheds with further examples of the many Standard classes being allocated to Scottish sheds from 1953 onward until construction ceased during 1957.

This increasing number of new Standard types led to the disposal of many older locomotives, so much so that by January 1957 the last working example of a Highland Railway-owned locomotive had been withdrawn and by April 1960 the last two examples of Great North of Scotland Railway locomotive power were also withdrawn from service. A large number of ex-Caledonian and North British locomotives extant in 1948, survived into the early 1960s but increasingly their numbers dwindled with the last Caley locomotive being withdrawn during 1963 and the last two NBR locomotives ending their service in June 1967 as previously noted.

From the late 1940s and early 1950s enthusiasts from England, in increasing numbers, would make the long journey north in what became known as the 'Grand Tour' to see the last examples of these rare classes before they became extinct. Fortunately many of these enthusiasts carried cameras to record these locomotives and together with local Scottish enthusiasts were, by the early 1960s, witnessing long lines of these veteran locomotives at sheds and dumps throughout Scotland awaiting their removal to the scrapyard.

This book is laid out in chronological order so that the reader may view the change in steam locomotive power from some of those early examples to the more modern classes of the LNER, LMSR and the BR Standard types that operated in Scotland.

ACKNOWLEDGEMENTS

Thanks are due to Tony Brown, Michael Mensing and Stuart Sellar for the use of their photographs and their assistance with details for captioning. I would also like to thank Richard Barber of the Armstrong Railway Photographic Trust (ARPT) and Colin Stacey of Initial Photographics for their attention to the detail in supplying photographs from their respective collections. Thanks also go to David Ball for access to his father's collection of photographs.

Saturday 19 June 1948. Still wearing garter blue livery, ex-LNER Class A4 4–6–2 no. 60012 *Commonwealth of Australia* simmers at Haymarket shed in Edinburgh. Built at Doncaster Works in 1937, this locomotive would be allocated to Haymarket for almost its entire working life only moving to Ferryhill in Aberdeen during January 1964 to become one of the locomotives rostered to work the fast three-hour services between Glasgow and Aberdeen. Withdrawal was to follow shortly afterwards in August 1964. *(A.C.J. Ball)*

Saturday 19 June 1948. The ex-LNER Class D11 4–4–0 was a development of the GCR 'Director' Class 11E (LNER Class D10) designed by J.G. Robinson. Locomotives of part two of the class were constructed specifically to the North British Railway loading gauge and they worked on the fast inter-city expresses between Edinburgh and Glasgow and services to Fife and Dundee. Seen at Haymarket shed in Edinburgh, no. 62671 *Bailie MacWheeble* had been built by Kitson & Co. in 1924 and was the first of the D11/2 version to appear in July of that year. She would be withdrawn from service during May 1961. This locomotive was named after a character in the 1814 novel *Waverley* by Sir Walter Scott. *(A.C.J. Ball)*

Saturday 19 June 1948. This photograph illustrates the situation prevailing during the first few years of Nationalisation, with many locomotives waiting for entry into the workshops before they could acquire their new identities. At St Margarets shed in Edinburgh, ex-NBR Class G (LNER Class Y9) 0–4–0 saddle tank no. 8092 (left) still retains its LNER identity, while sister locomotive no. 68097 (right) gleams in its new British Railways livery. Built for shunting duties in docks and small sidings, examples of this class could be seen working in Leith and Dundee docks. No. 8092 was effectively the first of the class to be constructed by Neilson & Co. during 1882 and she would be withdrawn (as 68092) in February 1953 after seventy-one years of service. No. 68097, constructed at Cowlairs Works in 1887, would survive until October 1958, having served the same number of years. *(A.C.J. Ball)*

Tuesday 22 June 1948. Seen here at Mallaig shed is ex-GNR Class H3 (LNER Class K2) 2–6–0 no. 1789 *Loch Laidon*. The photographer noted that it would depart with the 1.00 p.m. service to Fort William consisting of four corridor coaches and six fish vans. Built by Kitson & Co. in 1921 and allocated to Eastfield shed in Glasgow in the mid-1920s, she would be withdrawn in September 1959. *(A.C.J. Ball)*

Wednesday 23 June 1948. Designed by W.P. Reid for the North British Railway and introduced in 1913, the 'Glen' Class K (LNER Class D34) 4–4–0s were primarily intended to work the West Highland line to Fort William and its extension to Mallaig. The majority of these powerful, superheated locomotives were thus based at Eastfield shed in Glasgow, although smaller allocations were to be found in Edinburgh and Fife. This photograph shows 1913-constructed no. 2469 *Glen Douglas*, still in LNER livery, waiting at Alloa station at the head of a passenger train. In 1959 this locomotive would be restored to its NBR livery (reverting to its NBR number, 256) and used on special workings until 1965 when it was retired to the Glasgow Museum of Transport. *(A.C.J. Ball)*

Wednesday 23 June 1948. Standing at Stirling shed is ex-NBR Class B (LNER Class J37) 0–6–0 no. 4544. Yet to acquire its British Railways number, 64544, it bears all the pre-Nationalisation identity marks. The front buffer-beam shows its number, class and depot allocation – Stirling. The B Class were the non-superheated sisters of the S Class and were identical in appearance, both types having been designed by W.P. Reid and introduced during 1914. This locomotive, built in 1915, would survive until December 1962. *(A.C.J. Ball)*

Thursday 24 June 1948. In grimy condition and still bearing its LMS identity, 'Small Ben' (LMS Class 2P) 4–4–0 no. 14409 *Ben Alisky* stands outside Helmsdale shed. Constructed by the Highland Railway at its Lochgorm Works in Inverness during 1900 to a Peter Drummond design from 1898, this locomotive was one of a class of twenty examples built primarily for main line passenger duties on the lines north of Inverness. By the time of its withdrawal in April 1950 it would be one of only five still working. Unfortunately, the last survivor, no. 54398 *Ben Alder*, withdrawn during 1953 and stored until 1966, was sent for scrap. *(A.C.J. Ball)*

Thursday 24 June 1948. Photographed at Forres shed, ex-HR 'Loch' (LMS Class 2P) 4–4–0 no. 14385 *Loch Tay* was the last survivor of a class of eighteen locomotives designed by David Jones and constructed by Dübs & Co. in 1896, primarily for express passenger traffic on the Highland main line between Perth and Inverness. Displaced by the larger Highland 4–6–0 designs, they were relegated to secondary duties. This locomotive would be withdrawn from service at Forres in April 1950. Rebuilt by the LMS in the form seen here during 1928, she would lose the distinctive tall louvred chimney and smokebox wing plates, somewhat diminishing her original attractive lines. *(A.C.J. Ball)*

Thursday 24 June 1948. Still bearing its green livery and obviously well cared for by the shed staff at Keith, ex-GER Class S69 (LNER Class B12) 4–6–0 no. 61503 awaits its next duty at Elgin shed. Built at Stratford Works in 1912, this locomotive was one of five examples of the class transferred in 1931 within the LNER to Scotland to work the GNoSR section. As the decade progressed they were followed by others of the class allocated either to Keith or Kittybrewster in Aberdeen. This example would be withdrawn during May 1951. *(A.C.J. Ball)*

Friday 25 June 1948. It is generally accepted that the Great North of Scotland Railway built some of the most graceful 4–4–0 locomotives ever to work in Great Britain. Lending credence to that view is this photograph of Class V no. 2262 taken at Keith shed, showing the graceful curve of the splashers; the slender, slightly tapering chimney and the tall dome of this William Pickersgill design of 1899. Classified D40 by the LNER, the locomotive still proudly wears that company's identity. Built by Neilson Reid & Co. in 1899, it was the first numerically in the class and it would remain in service until October 1955. *(A.C.J. Ball)*

Sunday 27 June 1948. This general view of Alloa shed shows the two-road building and its rudimentary facilities, an outdoor overhead gantry crane and a couple of grounded coach bodies serving as crew restrooms. Completing the picture is ex-NBR Class B (LNER Class J35) 0–6–0 no. 4497 together with an unidentified classmate. Constructed as an unsuperheated locomotive by the North British Locomotive Co. (NBL) during 1909, she would be rebuilt with a superheated boiler in 1932 and survive a further thirty years only to be withdrawn from service during April 1962. *(K.H. Cockerill/ARPT)*

Friday 13 August 1948. The heavy storms that took place throughout East Lothian and Berwickshire on 12 August 1948 filled the rivers draining from the Lammermuir Hills and caused tremendous damage to the East Coast Main Line between Grantshouse and Reston, washing out many bridges and embankments and closing the line for three months. The result was that all traffic to Edinburgh had to be diverted and the Tweed Valley line and the Waverley Route carried the bulk of this re-routing. It also meant that locomotives were drafted in from other regions to assist with additional movements, and here we see ex-WD Class 8F 2–8–0 no. 63182 (ex-WD no. 79185) passing St Margarets shed with a train of empty coaching stock from Craigentinny to Waverley station. Allocated to 51B Newport shed she was still carrying her LNER number that would be changed to 90503 by British Railways. Built by the Vulcan Foundry in 1944 she would see service in northern Europe towards the end of the Second World War and be sold to the LNER at the end of 1946. Purchased by British Railways during 1948 she would be withdrawn from service in January 1967. *(B.W.L Brooksbank/Initial Photographics)*

Friday 20 August 1948. The ex-NBR Class J (LNER Class D30) 4–4–0s were the first of the W.P. Reid-designed locomotives to be fitted with superheaters. The twenty-seven engines of the class were constructed between 1912 and 1920 and were named after characters from the novels of Sir Walter Scott. Known as 'Superheated Scotts', we see here at Thornton shed no. 2430 *Jingling Geordie*, named after the character of George Heriot in Sir Walter Scott's 1822 novel *The Fortunes of Nigel*. This locomotive was built at Cowlairs Works during 1914 and it would be withdrawn in January 1957. *(A.G. Forsyth/Initial Photographics)*

Sunday 22 August 1948. Parked in the yard at Inverness depot is ex-HR 'Small Ben' (LMS Class 2P) 4–4–0 no. 14416 *Ben a'Bhuird*, it would be withdrawn from service during the same month. This locomotive was the final example of the class to be constructed by NBL during 1906 and she would be rebuilt in the form we see here by the LMS during 1929. Note the 32A shed code on the smokebox door, the LMS code for Inverness. *(B.W.L. Brooksbank/Initial Photographics)*

Wednesday 25 August 1948. Shunting in the yard at Dingwall station is ex-HR 'Small Ben' (LMS Class 2P) 4–4–0 no. 14401 *Ben Vrackie* looking in comparatively clean condition. This example of the class was built by Dübs & Co. during 1899, would be rebuilt by the LMS in 1930 and withdrawn two months after this photograph was taken in October 1948. Note the distinctive Dübs diamond-shaped builder's plate on the front splasher, also note the 'Tredegar' private owner wagon next to the locomotive, a long way from home. *(B.W.L. Brooksbank/Initial Photographics)*

Friday 20 May 1949. Over a period of years the LMS had transferred a number of Class 2P 4–4–0s to sheds in Scotland, primarily to supplement the ageing locomotives throughout the G&SWR territory. Seen at Hurlford shed is a rather grimy-looking no. 40665. Built at Derby Works during 1931 she appears to have been based at Hurlford for her entire working life and would be withdrawn from service in June 1962. This class was a Henry Fowler-designed variant of the earlier Johnson-designed Midland Railway Class 2s, having 6ft 9in driving wheels instead of 7ft. *(K.H. Cockerill/ARPT)*

Saturday 21 May 1949. Bearing her new identity is ex-NBR Class A (LNER Class N15) 0–6–2 tank no. 69203 parked in the yard at Stobcross. Built by Robert Stephenson & Co. in 1923 she would be withdrawn during June 1958. *(K.H. Cockerill/ARPT)*

Saturday 21 May 1949. Still bearing her LMS identity, Class 2F 0–6–0 tank no. 7169 is seen here in the yard at Greenock Princes Pier. Designed by Henry Fowler, these short wheelbase locomotives were primarily for work in dockyards. Constructed at Derby Works during 1928 and 1929, the class consisted of only ten locomotives, no. 7169 being built in 1929. She would be withdrawn thirty years later in September 1959. *(K.H. Cockerill/ARPT)*

Tuesday 24 May 1949. Seen here shunting in the yard at Brechin is ex-CR Class 439 (LMS Class 2P) 0–4–4 tank no. 15214. Looking well cared for by the staff at Forfar shed, her LMS identity is still in good condition. The driver is watching carefully as the shunter is 'in between' coupling up. This example of the class was built at St Rollox Works in 1912 and would serve for forty-nine years before being withdrawn during September 1961. *(K.H. Cockerill/ARPT)*

Saturday 18 June 1949. One of several types of 0–6–0 classes produced for the CR were the McIntosh designed Class 812 mixed traffic locomotives. A total of seventy-nine were constructed both at St Rollox Works and by three outside contractors – Neilson & Co., Dübs & Co. and Sharp Stewart & Co. Seen here at Ayr shed is no. 57614 still bearing the initials LMS on its tender. The class would be designated 3F by the LMS. This example was built at St Rollox in 1900 and would be withdrawn from service in October 1962. *(A.C.J. Ball)*

Saturday 18 June 1949. The ex-NBR Class S 0–6–0s were constructed with superheated boilers and were intended specifically to work heavy goods trains, especially the Fife coal trains. More than 100 were built between 1914 and 1921 and they became designated Class J37 by the LNER. These powerful locomotives were given the 5F classification by British Railways with virtually all of them surviving into the 1960s. This photograph taken at Ayr shed shows no. 64605, built by the NBL in 1919, and destined to be withdrawn during June 1964. *(A.C.J. Ball)*

Sunday 19 June 1949. Introduced from 1912, with building continuing until 1921, the twenty-three 0–6–0 tank locomotives of the CR 498 Class were officially designated 'Dock Tanks' but could also be found shunting in goods yards in the Glasgow and Edinburgh areas. Classified 2F by British Railways, no. 56158 sports its new identity at Yoker shed in Glasgow. Built in 1915 at St Rollox Works, it was to put in a total of forty-six years' service, not being withdrawn until January 1961. *(A.C.J. Ball)*

Sunday 19 June 1949. The ex-CR Class 782 0–6–0 tanks were larger in all respects than the Class 498s. Later classified 3F by British Railways, they were intended primarily for general shunting and short trip goods work. Construction commenced in 1895 and, together with the very similar Class 29, all 147 of them were constructed at St Rollox Works. Here we see no. 56339 looking smart in its new BR livery at Yoker shed in Glasgow; built in 1911 it would be withdrawn in August 1956. *(A.C.J. Ball)*

Monday 20 June 1949. Having only just been repainted in its new black British Railways livery, ex-CR Class 139 or 'Superheated Dunalastair IV' (LMS Class 3P) 4–4–0 no. 54452 rests between duties at Hurlford depot. Constructed from 1910 to 1914 at St Rollox Works, the twenty-two locomotives of this class represented the culmination of the McIntosh-designed 'Dunalastair' series. Used initially on express passenger trains throughout the Caledonian system, they were relegated to minor duties as larger LMS locomotives such as the Stanier 'Black 5' 4–6–0s were allocated to Scotland. This example was constructed in 1913 and would be withdrawn during July 1957. *(A.C.J. Ball)*

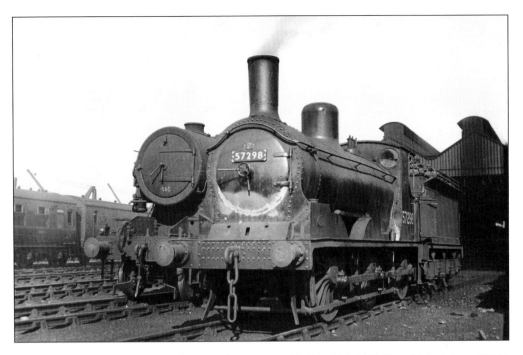

Friday 24 June 1949. Looking a little worse for wear, ex-CR Class 294 (LMS Class 2F) 0–6–0 no. 57298 stands on shed at Carstairs. A veteran of 1887, it was built at St Rollox Works to an 1883 design by Dugald Drummond. Its lines are somewhat spoilt here by the stovepipe chimney. Still bearing an LMS Carstairs 28C shed code, it would be among the earlier withdrawals of the class in April 1950. *(A.C.J. Ball)*

Friday 24 June 1949. One of a class of only seventeen engines, and designed by McIntosh, ex-CR Class 652 (LMS Class 3F) 0–6–0 no. 57635 stands at Carstairs shed showing the sturdy lines of a traditional Caledonian 0–6–0. Yet to be fitted with its smokebox numberplate, it still bears an LMS Carstairs 28C shed code. Constructed at St Rollox Works in 1908 it would be withdrawn during March 1962. *(A.C.J. Ball)*

Saturday 11 March 1950. Another Caley veteran is seen here at Stirling shed, ex-CR Class 711 (LMS Class 2F) 0–6–0 no. 57468 was a McIntosh-built period locomotive based on an original design by Dugald Drummond and constructed at St Rollox Works in 1897. She would be withdrawn during February 1952. *(C.J.B. Sanderson/ARPT)*

Saturday 11 March 1950. William Pickersgill designed only two classes of 4–6–0s for the Caledonian Railway, the most numerous of which was the two-cylinder Class 60 (LMS Class 4P) with twenty-six being constructed at St Rollox Works. Only the first six locomotives appeared in Caley days with the LMS building a further twenty during 1925 and 1926. Seen here at Stirling is no. 14645, one of the 1926 batch that would be withdrawn four months after this photograph, in July 1950. *(C.J.B. Sanderson/ARPT)*

Saturday 6 May 1950. One of only two constructed, ex-LNER Class V4 2–6–2 no. 61700 *Bantam Cock* is seen here at Eastfield shed in Glasgow. Designed by Nigel Gresley in 1939, the pair were built at Doncaster Works during 1941 and seen as a lighter weight version of the successful Class V2 locomotives therefore giving a greater route availability. Allocated to Eastfield in Glasgow they would be seen regularly working on the West Highland route to Fort William and Mallaig. During 1954 both locomotives would be transferred to Aberdeen and saw regular work out of both Ferryhill and Kittybrewster sheds. This example would be withdrawn from service during March 1957. *(C.J.B. Sanderson/ARPT)*

Friday 12 May 1950. After Nationalisation many locomotives were hurriedly given their new numbers but retained their old company identities for a while. One example was ex-NBR Class L (LNER Class C16) 4–4–2 tank no. 67497, seen here at Penicuik still bearing the letters LNER on her tankside. Constructed by the NBL during 1921, she would spend almost her entire working life based at St Margarets shed in Edinburgh and was utilised initially on the services to Dunbar and latterly on the Penicuik branch. She would be withdrawn during October 1959. The Penicuik branch was opened by the Penicuik Railway in September 1872 but was operated by the NBR from the outset. Although offering a sparse passenger service, the branch's main source of revenue was traffic from the many paper mills dotted along the banks of the River North Esk. Passenger services were withdrawn in September 1951 but there was still a twice-daily goods service for paper mill traffic up to the final closure during March 1967. Most of the former trackbed is now a footpath and cycleway. *(C.J.B. Sanderson/ARPT)*

June 1950. One of the earliest of the Nigel Gresley designs of 1914 is shown here – ex-GNR Class J23 (LNER Class J50) 0–6–0 tank no. 68953 was of post-grouping construction at Doncaster Works during 1926. Allocated new to Eastfield shed (one of only a handful of the class to be allocated directly to Scotland), she survived working in Glasgow goods yards until being withdrawn during July 1959. *(C.J.B. Sanderson/ARPT)*

Opposite, top: **June 1950**. Looking resplendent ex-works in her new British Railways livery of plain black is ex-NBR Class D (LNER Class J83) 0–6–0 tank no. 68479. Careful observation of the smokebox top will reveal the pulley attachment fitted for use with a slip coupling release cable as fitted to those locomotives used for banking from Glasgow Queen Street station up the notorious Cowlairs Bank. Constructed by Sharp Stewart & Co. during 1901, she would serve for sixty-two years before being withdrawn in October 1962. *(C.J.B. Sanderson/ARPT)*

Opposite, bottom: **Saturday 3 June 1950**. One of the most powerful 4–4–0 classes to be utilised over the old LNER system in Scotland were the Nigel Gresley-designed, three-cylinder 'Shires' or Class D49. Seen here at Dundee Tay Bridge shed is no. 62709 *Berwickshire*. Built at Darlington Works during 1928 she would be withdrawn from service in January 1960. *(C.J.B. Sanderson/ARPT)*

Sunday 4 June 1950. Ex-GER Class S69 (LNER Class B12) 4–6–0 no. 61507 was constructed at Stratford Works during 1913 and would be transferred to the GNoSR section of the LNER during 1940. Seen here at Kittybrewster shed in Aberdeen, she was an example of the class to be rebuilt with a round-top boiler, others were constructed with Belpaire fireboxes. She would be withdrawn in February 1953. *(C.J.B. Sanderson/ARPT)*

Sunday 4 June 1950. Bearing her new number but lacking a company identity, ex-NBR Class A (LNER Class N14) 0–6–2 tank no. 69125 has just had her bunker filled with coal at Kittybrewster shed. Built by the NBL during 1909 she would be withdrawn in March 1954. *(C.J.B. Sanderson/ARPT)*

Monday 12 June 1950. Appearing to float on a sea of empty fish boxes, ex-LNER Class K4 2–6–0 no. 61998 *MacLeod of MacLeod* sits in the sidings at the harbour in Mallaig waiting for fish vans to be loaded. Constructed at Darlington Works in 1938 and entering traffic during January 1939 she was originally numbered 3446 and named *Lord of Dunvegan* for a few months before receiving her final name. This photograph shows her still sporting LNER green livery but with British Railways on the tender. Allocated new to Glasgow Eastfield shed to work the West Highland line, she spent the bulk of her working life on this route before being withdrawn from service late in 1961 when based at Thornton shed. *(R.J. Buckley/Initial Photographics)*

Monday 10 July 1950. Bearing A Class lamps, ex-LNER Class V1 2–6–2 tank no. 67609 has paused at the Up platform at Hawick station with an inspection saloon in tow. Constructed at Doncaster Works during 1931 she would be rebuilt as a Class V3 locomotive in 1953 and withdrawn from service in February 1962. Allocated new to Eastfield shed in Glasgow, by the time of this photograph she was based at St Margarets shed in Edinburgh. *(C.J.B. Sanderson/ARPT)*

Monday 10 July 1950. At the head of a local stopper, ex-NBR Class J 'Superheated Scott' (LNER Class D30) 4–4–0 no. 62422 *Caleb Balderstone*, pauses at the southbound platform at Hawick station. Constructed at Cowlairs Works in 1914, she was named after the butler character in the 1819 Scott novel *The Bride of Lammermoor* and be withdrawn during December 1958. All of the railway infrastructure in this scene was to be swept away after the closure of the Waverley Route in January 1969. *(C.J.B. Sanderson/ARPT)*

Monday 10 July 1950. Bearing her new British Railways identity but in LNER green livery, Edinburgh Waverley station pilot locomotive ex-NBR Class D (LNER Class J83) 0–6–0 tank no. 68481 is seen here at rest outside Haymarket shed. The last of the class to be constructed by Sharp Stewart & Co. during 1901, she would be withdrawn in February 1962. *(C.J.B. Sanderson/ARPT)*

Thursday 3 August 1950. This photograph of ex-GER Class M15 (LNER Class F4) 2–4–2 tank no. 67157 clearly shows the slightly awkward-looking lines of the class introduced by T.W. Worsdell during 1884. This example was constructed at Stratford Works in 1907 and was sent north in 1948 to work the St Combs branch. With a very light axle weight, she was one of only four members of the class to be sent to Scotland, all of which eventually found their way to work at some time or other on the St Combs branch from Fraserburgh. No. 67157 would eventually become the works pilot at Inverurie and would be the last of the class to be withdrawn during June 1956. *(A.G. Forsyth/Initial Photographics)*

Wednesday 4 October 1950. At Kittybrewster shed in Aberdeen ex-GER Class S69 (LNER Class B12) 4–6–0 no. 61503 is being prepared for duty by her driver. This Belpaire firebox-example of the class would be transferred to the GNoSR section of the LNER during 1931 and would be withdrawn twenty years later in 1951. *(K.H. Cockerill/ARPT)*

Saturday 21 April 1951. The driver and fireman of ex-GNoSR Class V (LNER Class D40) 4–4–0 no. 62269 are busy trimming the coal in the tender prior to departing from Craigellachie station with a train for Grantown-on-Spey. Designed by William Pickersgill, this example of the class was a rare example of an Inverurie Works-constructed locomotive that entered service during 1913. She would be withdrawn in September 1955. Note that the tender is fitted with a shelter to give additional protection to the crew during adverse weather conditions. *(C.J.B. Sanderson/ARPT)*

Opposite, top: **Sunday 8 October 1950**. South Leith shed was a sub-shed of St Margarets in Edinburgh and supplied locomotives for work in the yards around Leith docks. Seen standing in the shed yard is ex-NBR Class F (LNER Class J88) 0–6–0 tank no. 8325 still wearing, more than two years after Nationalisation, her LNER identity. Constructed at Cowlairs Works during 1905 she would give fifty-six years' service before being withdrawn in March 1961. *(K.H. Cockerill/ARPT)*

Opposite, bottom: **Wednesday 18 April 1951**. Still in LNER green livery but bearing her British Railways identity, ex-GER Class S69 (LNER Class B12) 4–6–0 no. 61539 is parked in the yard at Kittybrewster shed. She was constructed at Stratford Works during 1917 and was one of the early arrivals in the area having been sent from the south of England during 1933 to supplement the locomotive power over the GNoSR section. She would be withdrawn in November 1954. *(C.J.B. Sanderson/ARPT)*

Tuesday 24 April 1951. Sitting on the turntable at Inverness shed is an example of one of the rarer Highland Railway classes. The Christopher Cumming-designed 'Superheated Goods' class consisted of only eight locomotives constructed by Hawthorn Leslie & Co. of Newcastle during 1918 and 1919. More commonly known as 'Clan Goods', this example, no. 57956, has her new number but still bears the LMS motto on her tender. Classified by the LMS as 5F, these powerful locomotives were just as able working passenger traffic as they were on heavy good trains. She would be withdrawn from service just over a year later during May 1952. *(C.J.B. Sanderson/ARPT)*

Opposite, top: **Wednesday 25 April 1951**. Ex-HR 'Small Ben' Class (LMS Class 2P) 4–4–0 no. 54398 *Ben Alder* had been built by Dübs & Co. during 1898 and she would be withdrawn from service in February 1953 and reserved for possible preservation. Here we see her at Thurso station prior to departing with the branch train to Georgemas Junction. After withdrawal the locomotive was stored for long periods of time at various sheds throughout Scotland awaiting a decision about its future. It was finally to be seen at the back of Dawsholm shed in Glasgow before being sent for scrap in 1966. *(C.J.B. Sanderson/ARPT)*

Opposite, bottom: **Saturday 21 July 1951**. This overall view of Hawick shed captures the atmosphere of this busy borders country depot. Ex-NBR Class J 'Superheated Scott' (LNER Class D30) 4–4–0 no. 62423 *Dugald Dalgetty* sits in the foreground with two Class K moguls and a Class J35 in the background. The eagle-eyed observer will spot the horse and cart standing in the station forecourt. This scene would be completely swept away after the closure of the line during January 1969 and the site is now occupied by the Teviotdale Leisure Centre. *(C.J.B. Sanderson/ARPT)*

Saturday 28 July 1951. In glistening ex-works condition, ex-GCR Class 11F (LNER Class D11/2) 4–4–0 no. 62674 *Flora MacIvor* is seen parked in the yard at Eastfield shed in Glasgow. Built by Kitson & Co. in 1924 she would initially be allocated to Haymarket shed in Edinburgh but in later years was based at Eastfield. She was withdrawn in July 1961. Her name was based on a character from the 1814 novel *Waverley* by Sir Walter Scott. *(C.J.B. Sanderson/ARPT)*

Saturday 28 July 1951. Photographs of the only known ex-LNER owned Sentinel locomotive to work in Scotland are rare but luckily the photographer has managed to capture this image of Class Y1 no. 68138. This single speed Sentinel was purchased by the LNER in 1927 and spent her entire working life in Scotland. Allocated to Hawick but sub-shedded to Kelso to work the busy yard there, she ended her days at Ayr shed before being withdrawn in January 1959. *(C.J.B. Sanderson/ARPT)*

Sunday 13 April 1952. Ex-NBR Class D (LNER Class J83) 0–6–0 tank no. 68474 is looking rather forlorn and dust-covered outside the old NBR works at St Margarets in Edinburgh. Built by Sharp Stewart & Co. during 1901, this locomotive was to become one of the regular Waverley station pilots until withdrawal in April 1958. *(F. W. Hampson/ARPT)*

Sunday 13 April 1952. At the opposite side of Edinburgh to the previous photograph, a much cleaner ex-NBR Class D (LNER Class J83) 0–6–0 tank no. 68460 is seen at Haymarket shed. Built by Neilson Reid & Co., she entered service during 1901 and was withdrawn in November 1958. Another Waverley station pilot, she bears an LNER identity but sports a British Railways number. *(F. W. Hampson/ARPT)*

Monday 11 August 1952. In immaculate external condition and waiting to depart from Ballater station with a passenger train for Aberdeen, is ex-GER Class S69 (LNER Class B12) 4–6–0 no. 61563, wearing a Kittybrewster shed code. Constructed at Stratford Works in 1920 and sent to Scotland during 1939, she would remain in service for only a further eight months before being withdrawn in April 1953. The Ballater branch was opened in three stages between 1853 and 1866 and followed, for most of its route, the course of the River Dee. On what became known as 'Royal Deeside' the railway provided access for royal trains to Ballater and the subsequent journey forward by road to Balmoral Castle. *(A.G. Forsyth/Initial Photographics)*

Tuesday 12 August 1952. Still bearing an Edinburgh St Margarets shed code but by now sporting a cowcatcher is Class 2MT 2–6–0 no. 46460 having just arrived at St Combs with the branch train from Fraserburgh. This class of locomotive superseded the veteran Class F4 2–4–2 tanks before themselves being made redundant by DMUs. Designed by H.G. Ivatt and introduced during 1946, this example of the class was constructed at Crewe Works in 1950 and she would be withdrawn in August 1966. *(A.G. Forsyth/Initial Photographics)*

Wednesday 13 August 1952. Purchased from Manning Wardle & Co. during 1915, this ex-GNoSR Class X (LNER Class Z4) 0–4–2 tank no. 68191, seen here in the dock area, was one of two examples of the class of slightly lighter weight, purchased for shunting around Aberdeen harbour. Two companion locomotives of slightly heavier weight (GNoSR Class Y – LNER Class Z5) had been purchased earlier in 1915 and all four were used around the harbour until withdrawn, this example going for scrap in March 1959. *(A.G. Forsyth/Initial Photographics)*

Friday 15 August 1952. Waiting patiently for the right of way at Craigellachie station is ex-GNoSR Class T (LNER Class D41) 4–4–0 no. 62248 with a train for Boat of Garten. Built by Neilson & Co. and entering service during 1897 (when William Pickersgill was Locomotive Superintendent at the GNoSR), it was based at Keith shed for most of its working life and would be withdrawn two months after this photograph. *(A.G. Forsyth/Initial Photographics)*

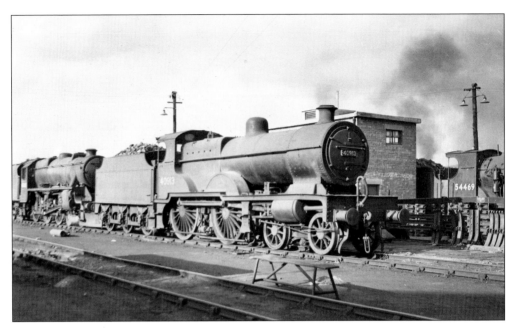

Friday 3 April 1953. Ex-LMS Class 4P 4–4–0 three-cylinder compound no. 40913 is seen here at Perth shed. Built at the Vulcan Foundry during 1927 she would be withdrawn in August 1955. This was another Henry Fowler-designed variation of a Midland Railway Johnson-designed class of locomotive, using 6ft 9in driving wheels instead of Johnson's 7ft. *(F.W. Hampson/ARPT)*

Sunday 19 April 1953. Two months after being withdrawn from service, ex-HR 'Small Ben' Class (LMS Class 2P) 4–4–0 no. 54398 *Ben Alder* is seen here parked in the yard beside Inverness shed. She would spend thirteen years in storage at various sheds before being scrapped. *(C.J.B. Sanderson/ARPT)*

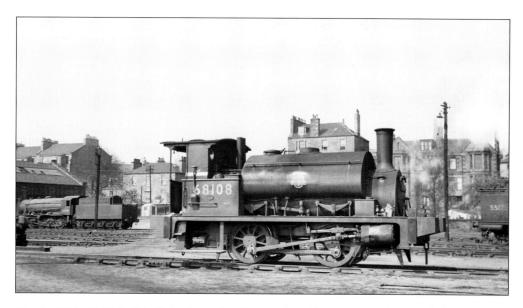

Monday 20 April 1953. This diminutive but well-proportioned locomotive parked in Dundee West shed yard is ex-NBR Class G (LNER Class Y9) 0–4–0 saddle tank no. 68108. Built at Cowlairs Works in 1890 she would be withdrawn during November 1959. Note the shunting step and handrail convenient for the shunters and the handy position of the shovel for the fireman. A total of thirty-eight of these little shunters would be built over a period of seventeen years. *(C.J.B. Sanderson/ARPT)*

Saturday 25 April 1953. Seen here at Parkhead shed is yet another locomotive still sporting its previous owner's identity but bearing its new British Railways number. In this instance it's ex-GNR Class H3 (LNER Class K2) 2–6–0 no. 61772 *Loch Lochy*, built by Kitson & Co. in 1921; she would be withdrawn during November 1959. Allocated to Eastfield shed in Glasgow during the early 1930s she was used primarily on the West Highland route and, along with other members of the class working to Fort William and Mallaig, was named during 1933 after a loch along the route. *(C.J.B. Sanderson/ARPT)*

Monday 22 June 1953. Picking up speed at the head of a Glasgow-bound express near Ferryhill in Aberdeen is BR Standard Class 5MT 4-6-0 no. 73007. Bearing a 63A Perth shed code and fitted with a small snowplough, she looks in good condition. Built at Derby Works during 1951 she was allocated new to Perth shed and would be withdrawn in March 1966. The Standard Class 5s were to all intents very able successors to the Stanier 'Black 5s', with 172 examples constructed by both Derby and Doncaster Works over a period of six years from 1951 until 1957. *(R. Butterfield/Initial Photographics)*

Opposite, top: **Tuesday 23 June 1953**. Maud Junction was the starting point for the 16-mile branch to Fraserburgh which was opened during April 1865, the Dyce to Peterhead line having been opened three years earlier in July 1862. Although fish from both ports could be said to constitute the bulk of the goods traffic, meat (primarily beef) being carried to the large markets in Aberdeen was also a good source of revenue. Here, BR Standard Class 4MT 2-6-4 tank no. 80021, with a rake of cattle wagons in tow, has stopped at the north end of the station on the Fraserburgh branch to take water. Built at Brighton Works in 1951 she would be withdrawn during July 1964. *(R. Butterfield/Initial Photographics)*

Opposite, bottom: **Tuesday 23 June 1953**. Having been turned on the turntable at Fraserburgh shed, BR Standard Class 4MT 2-6-4 tank no. 80004 simmers between duties. Built in Derby she entered service during 1952 and would be withdrawn in May 1967. Note in the background the impressive granite stonework of Fraserburgh South Parish Church which was built in 1878, a full thirteen years after the railway opened in 1865. *(R. Butterfield/Initial Photographics)*

Wednesday 24 June 1953. The 'Princess Coronation' class of locomotives are generally accepted as being the finest of William Stanier's designs. Thirty-eight were constructed at Crewe Works over a period of eleven years from 1937 until 1948, of which twenty-four entered service with streamlining. These streamlined locomotives were primarily used on the prestige services between London and Glasgow. The example seen here on the turntable at Ferryhill shed in Aberdeen, no. 46225 *Duchess of Gloucester*, came out of Crewe Works during 1938 as a streamlined version, although this would be removed during 1947 which would leave the locomotive with the slightly sloping top to the smokebox. She would be withdrawn from service during September 1964. *(R. Butterfield/Initial Photographics)*

Opposite, top: **Friday 26 June 1953**. Looking in very good external condition, this Kyle of Lochalsh pilot locomotive is ex-CR Class 439 (LMS Class 2P) 0–4–4 tank no. 55216. She certainly is a credit to the staff at Kyle shed; note the horseshoe wedged into the top of the smokebox numberplate – a lucky charm for the crew? A product of St Rollox Works in 1912 she would be withdrawn during October 1961. *(R. Butterfield/Initial Photographics)*

Opposite, bottom: **Saturday 27 June 1953**. In the queue of bankers sitting behind the Down platform at Beattock station is the unusual sight of a Pacific tank locomotive in the form of ex-CR Class 944 (LMS Class 4P) 4–6–2 tank no. 55359. Designed by William Pickersgill and intended for use on the passenger traffic between Glasgow and the Clyde coast towns, the twelve examples of the class were delivered from the NBL during the First World War, March to May 1917. They were found more useful work during the war period and it was not until hostilities ceased that these locomotives finally did the work they were intended for. The one on show here was transferred to Beattock for banking duties around the time of Nationalisation and she was the last of her class to be withdrawn during October 1953. *(R. Butterfield/Initial Photographics)*

Saturday 27 June 1953. Seen here restarting a Manchester to Glasgow service from Beattock station Down platform, having picked up a banker, is ex-LMS Class 6P 'Jubilee' 4–6–0 no. 45712 *Victory*. Built at Crewe Works in 1936 she would be withdrawn during November 1963. The William Stanier-designed Class 5XP or 'Jubilee' were initially lacklustre in their performance but after early trials with an improved form of superheater, these locomotives gained much better steaming qualities and an improved performance. *(R. Butterfield/Initial Photographics)*

Saturday 27 June 1953. Seen here at Moffat station, having just arrived with the branch train from the junction at Beattock, is ex-CR Class '439' (LMS Class 2P) 0–4–4 tank no. 55234. Based on a design stretching back to 1895, this example of the class was constructed at St Rollox Works during 1922 and would be withdrawn from service in December 1962. The short, 2-mile-long branch dated from 1883 when the daily service was thirteen trains which by 1951 was still a generous ten trains each way per weekday. Passenger services would be withdrawn during December 1954 but goods services would continue for a further ten years to be withdrawn in April 1964. *(R. Butterfield/Initial Photographics)*

Tuesday 4 August 1953. Ex-LNER Class A3 4–6–2 no. 60041 *Salmon Trout* is seen here climbing Cockburnspath Bank with the Up 'Queen of Scots Pullman'. Built at Doncaster Works in 1934, she was named after the 1924 St Leger winner and allocated new to Haymarket shed in Edinburgh. Seen here prior to being fitted with a double chimney and smoke deflectors, by 1960 she would be based at St Margarets shed and would be withdrawn from service in December 1965. *(C.J.B. Sanderson/ARPT)*

Monday 10 August 1953. Yet another sighting of the 'Queen of Scots Pullman' climbing the bank at Cockburnspath, this time with Class A2 4–6–2 no. 60534 *Irish Elegance* at its head. Designed by A.H. Peppercorn and built at Doncaster Works in 1948, she would be allocated to Haymarket shed in Edinburgh from 1949 until 1961 when she moved to St Margarets. Named after the 1919 winner of the Royal Hunt Cup, she was withdrawn during December 1962. *(C.J.B Sanderson/ARPT)*

Saturday 16 January 1954. Pausing while shunting in Newington Goods yard is ex-NBR Class S (LNER Class J37) 0–6–0 no. 64590 looking in good external condition. Designed by W.P. Reid as a superheated class of goods locomotives, this engine was built by the NBL during 1918 and she was withdrawn in May 1962. *(W.S. Sellar)*

Saturday 14 August 1954. One of the pair of resident west end pilots at Waverley station is busying itself with moving empty coaching stock. Ex-NBR Class D (LNER Class J83) 0–6–0 tank no. 68478 is seen here in plain black livery. Constructed by Sharp Stewart & Co. during 1901, she would be withdrawn from service in November 1958. *(F.W. Hampson/ARPT)*

Wednesday 1 September 1954. Standing beside the water tank at Kipps shed in Glasgow is ex-GNR Class N2 (LNER Class N2) 0–6–2 tank no. 69518. Designed by Nigel Gresley and built by the NBL in 1921, she would be based new at King's Cross shed in London from where she would be transferred to Glasgow during 1927 to work on the suburban services around that city. They were not greatly loved by the Scottish crews and owing to their heavy axle weight they were banned from some Scottish branch lines with this example being withdrawn in January 1961. *(G. Forsyth/Initial Photographics)*

Saturday 12 February 1955. On this cold February day with the remains of a recent snowfall on the ground, ex-LMS Class 4P 4–4–0 three-cylinder compound no. 40938 prepares to depart from Callander station with the Saturdays-only 1.25 p.m. stopping service to Stirling. Constructed at Derby Works during 1932 as the penultimate member of the class, this locomotive was an LMS post-grouping development of the successful Midland Railway compound 4–4–0s. She was withdrawn in July 1956. *(W.S. Sellar)*

Saturday 12 March 1955. Entering Morningside Road station with an Edinburgh 'Inner Circle' suburban train is ex-LNER Class D49 4–4–0 no. 62712 *Morayshire*. Designed by Nigel Gresley and built at Darlington Works in 1928, she is a three-cylinder engine fitted with Walschaerts valve gear. She would be withdrawn during July 1961 and moved to Slateford laundry for use as a stationary boiler until January 1962 when she went into store and was subsequently purchased privately. She is currently based at the SRPS site at Bo'ness where she can be seen working. *(W.S. Sellar)*

Opposite, top: **Wednesday 4 May 1955**. Ex-LMS Class 4MT 2–6–4 tank no. 42269 is seen entering Merchiston station in Edinburgh while working a Carstairs to Edinburgh Princes Street service. Constructed at Derby Works during 1947, this class was a Charles Fairburn variation of an earlier William Stanier design. She would be withdrawn in July 1967. *(W.S. Sellar)*

Opposite, bottom: **Tuesday 17 May 1955**. Looking in very good condition, ex-CR 439 (LMS Class 2P) 0–4–4 tank no. 55202 is seen working a Leith North to Edinburgh Princes Street passenger train soon after leaving Craigleith station. Constructed at St Rollox Works in 1909 she would be withdrawn during August 1961. Passenger services on this branch commenced during the 1870s and survived to be dieselised during 1959, but the competition of Edinburgh Corporation buses was too much and passenger services ceased in April 1962 with goods services lingering on until August 1968. *(W.S. Sellar)*

Saturday 28 May 1955. On the turntable at Inverness roundhouse is a very clean example of William Stanier's successful design of Class 5 4–6–0 – the class known throughout the railway fraternity as the 'Black 5'. A total of 842 locomotives were constructed from their introduction in 1934 until 1951 when the last came into service. The locomotive seen here, no. 44722, was a product of Crewe Works during 1949 that would be withdrawn in April 1967. *(F.W. Hampson/ARPT)*

Saturday 28 May 1955. This smartly turned out locomotive at Elgin shed is ex-GNoSR Class V (LNER Class D40) 4–4–0 no. 62264. Designed by William Pickersgill and constructed by Neilson Reid & Co. during 1899, she would be withdrawn in March 1957. This photograph clearly shows the graceful lines of the class. *(F.W. Hampson/ARPT)*

Sunday 29 May 1955. Ex-GNR Class N2 (LNER Class N2) 0–6–2 tank no. 69562 sits in the yard at Parkhead shed. Sent north by the LNER when new to work suburban trains in the Glasgow area, she had been constructed at Doncaster Works in 1925 and would be withdrawn from service only eight months after this photograph was taken, during January 1956. *(F.W. Hampson/ARPT)*

Monday 30 May 1955. Almost dwarfed by the enormous water tank at Haymarket shed is ex-GCR Class 11F (LNER Class D11/2) 4–4–0 no. 62677 *Edie Ochiltree*. A post-grouping development of the 'Director' class these were specifically constructed to fit the ex-NBR loading gauge. This example was constructed by Kitson & Co. during 1924 and she was withdrawn in August 1959. *Edie Ochiltree* was named after the professional beggar character in Sir Walter Scott's 1816 novel, *The Antiquary*. *(F.W. Hampson/ARPT)*

Wednesday 15 June 1955. Ex-NBR Class B (LNER Class J37) 0–6–0 no. 64582 is seen approaching Morningside Road on the Edinburgh suburban 'Outer Circle' with a train of unfitted grain wagons. These LGW (Leith General Warehouseman) private owner wagons were used almost exclusively to carry grain from Leith docks to the maltings in the Gorgie and Slateford areas of Edinburgh. The locomotive was the product of the NBL in 1918 and survived over forty-five years before being withdrawn during November 1963. *(W.S. Sellar)*

Friday 24 June 1955. Seen here is an ex-Caledonian Railway greyhound, a Class 140 or 'Dunalastair IV' (LMS Class 3P) 4–4–0 built at St Rollox during 1908 as a saturated steam locomotive later to be rebuilt with a superheated boiler. With 6ft 6in driving wheels this class worked express passenger trains throughout the Caley system until replaced during LMS days by larger locomotives. One of only three examples of the class of nineteen locomotives to reach British Railways service, no. 54439 is seen standing outside Wick shed; she would be withdrawn during August 1958. *(R. Butterfield/Initial Photographics)*

Saturday 25 June 1955. Designed by Peter Drummond and built by the HR at their Lochgorm Works at Inverness during 1905 and 1906, the four diminutive examples of his 0–4–4 Class 'Passenger Tank' (LMS Class 0P) locomotives found service on the lightly laid branches of that railway. This one, no. 55051, was being used on the Dornoch branch and is seen here shunting in Mound station. She was withdrawn during June 1956. *(R. Butterfield/Initial Photographics)*

Saturday 25 June 1955. Seen standing in the yard at Inverness shed is ex-CR Pickersgill-designed Class 300 (LMS Class 3F) 0–6–0 no. 57661. Introduced during 1918, this would be the last class of Caledonian 0–6–0s to be built before the grouping. This example was a product of St Rollox Works in 1918 and would be withdrawn during September 1963. *(R. Butterfield/Initial Photographics)*

Saturday 2 July 1955. This photograph shows an earlier example of the Caledonian variety of 0–6–0 classes. Designed by Pickersgill's predecessor, John McIntosh, the Class 812 was introduced during 1899 and also classified as 3F by the LMS. This one, no. 57628, seen here at Ayr shed, was constructed at St Rollox Works during 1899 and would give sixty-one years of service before being withdrawn in February 1960. Note the British Railways shed code 67C – Ayr, positioned as per the LMS practice, on the upper part of the smokebox. *(R. Butterfield/Initial Photographics)*

Tuesday 26 July 1955. Seen here taking water in the yard at Kittybrewster shed in Aberdeen is BR Standard Class 4MT 2–6–4 tank no. 80107. A product of Doncaster Works in 1954, she was initially allocated to Polmadie shed in Glasgow but soon found her way to the north-east of Scotland to be based at Kittybrewster. She was withdrawn in September 1964. *(A.G. Forsyth/Initial Photographics)*

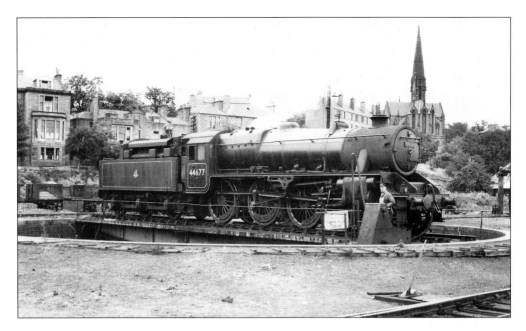

Friday 29 July 1955. Seen here on the turntable at Dundee West shed is Class 5 4–6–0 no. 44677. The fireman is busy trimming the coal in the self-weighing tender. Built at Horwich Works in 1950 she would be withdrawn during October 1967. The distinctive landmark in the background is the delicate-looking spire of Dundee West church constructed during the early 1880s. *(A.G. Forsyth/Initial Photographics)*

Monday 5 September 1955. Approaching Morningside Road with an Edinburgh 'Inner Circle' suburban service, is ex-LNER Class V1 2–6–2 tank no. 67666. Built at Doncaster Works and entering service during August 1938 as a class V1 locomotive, she would be rebuilt as a class V3 in January 1961, only to be withdrawn in February 1962. *(W.S. Sellar)*

Saturday 17 September 1955. Following the retirement of John McIntosh from the Caledonian Railway in 1924, William Pickersgill succeeded him as Locomotive Superintendent and proceeded to build on the success of the Dunalastair series of 4–4–0s designed by McIntosh. Introduced from 1916, a total of forty-eight examples of these robust locomotives were built over a period of six years up to 1922 by a variety of manufacturers, including the NBL and Armstrong Whitworth & Co. and of course the CR itself at its St Rollox Works. Here we see ex-CR Class 72 (LMS Class 3P) no. 54494 at Ladybank station waiting to depart with the last train to Perth via the Newburgh route. Built by Armstrong Whitworth & Co. in 1921, she would be withdrawn during August 1960. With a service of only two trains per day through this sparsely populated country area, it is hardly surprising that the branch was an early closure. *(W.S. Sellar)*

Opposite: **Monday 12 September 1955**. At the head of a train of loaded, unfitted coal wagons, ex-NBR Class C (LNER Class J36) 0–6–0 no. 65225 has a full head of steam but is blowing badly as she slogs her way up the rising gradient from Craiglockhart to Morningside Road on the Edinburgh 'Inner Circle' suburban line. Constructed at Cowlairs Works in 1891, this veteran would be rebuilt in the form we see here during 1917 and was finally withdrawn after sixty-six years of service in October 1957. *(W.S. Sellar)*

Monday 19 September 1955. The W.P. Reid-designed ex-NBR Class L (LNER Class C16) 4–4–2 tanks were the superheated version of the same designers Class M (LNER Class C15) locomotives. Allocated mainly to Edinburgh and Glasgow sheds for the suburban work around those cities, they were superseded by both the Class N2 and Class V1/V3 locomotives and were relegated to minor lines and duties. On this day at Hawick shed we see, above, no. 67489 and, below, no. 67495. The complete class of twenty-one locomotives were built by the NBL with the two shown here entering traffic early in 1916. No. 67489 would be withdrawn during February 1961 while no. 67495 had been withdrawn in May 1956. *(Both W.S. Sellar)*

Monday 17 October 1955. Delivered new to Haymarket shed in Edinburgh from Doncaster Works during 1947, ex-LNER Class A2/3 4–6–2 no. 60519 *Honeyway* would spend most of her working life based at that shed working traffic to Newcastle, Carlisle, Perth and Dundee. She is seen here at Niddrie North Junction with a service to Carlisle which will traverse the Waverley Route. Named after the 1946 Champion Stakes winner, she had a relatively short working life of only fifteen years before being withdrawn in December 1962. *(W.S. Sellar)*

Wednesday 19 October 1955. Seen here with a coal train from Duddingston Yard, ex-NBR Class B (LNER Class J35) 0–6–0 no. 64486 is starting its charge up the 1 in 30 gradient to St Leonards Yard in the city of Edinburgh. Built by the NBL during 1909 in an unsuperheated form, it would be rebuilt with a superheated boiler in 1931 and serve just short of fifty years, being withdrawn in September 1958. The St Leonards branch had a long history being part of Edinburgh's first railway, the Edinburgh and Dalkeith Railway, a horse-drawn tramway built to a gauge of 4ft 6in and opened in 1831. Built to carry coal into the city it was purchased by the NBR in 1845 and converted to standard gauge during 1847, the same year passenger traffic ceased. This branch not only supplied the coal yard but served a whisky bottling plant, a brewery and a large print works. It was closed during 1968 and the trackbed now forms part of a cycleway. *(W.S. Sellar)*

Saturday 19 May 1956. Ex-CR Class 294 (LMS Class 2F) 0–6–0 no. 57357 is seen here at Ardrossan shed. Built at St Rollox Works during 1892, she would be withdrawn in March 1962 after seventy years of service. *(F.W. Hampson/ARPT)*

Saturday 19 May 1956. Seen here at Muirkirk shed is LMS Class 4F 0–6–0 no. 44281. A 1926 product of Derby Works, she would be withdrawn in December 1962. Allocated to Hurlford shed 67B, Muirkirk was a sub-shed that lay within the Lanarkshire coalfield and supplied motive power for the traffic from the collieries there. *(F.W. Hampson/ARPT)*

Saturday 19 May 1956. The classic 'Caley Bogie', a Pickersgill Class 72 (LMS Class 3P) 4–4–0 no. 54505 seen here at Carstairs shed. Constructed by the NBL during 1922 she would be withdrawn in April 1961. *(F.W. Hampson/ARPT)*

Monday 21 May 1956. At St Rollox Works, ex-CR Class 72 (LMS Class 3P) 4–4–0 no. 54500 has been overhauled and repainted in her new British Railways livery and the number transfers are being applied to the cabside. Another product of the NBL during 1922, she would be withdrawn from service during 1962. *(F.W. Hampson/ARPT)*

Saturday 26 May 1956. Waiting for her next duty at Haymarket shed, ex-LNER Class B1 4–6–0 no. 61081 looks relatively clean. Built by the NBL during 1946 she would be withdrawn after only eighteen years of service in June 1964. Designed by Edward Thompson immediately after taking office in 1941 following the sudden death of Sir Nigel Gresley in April of that year, the 410 members of the class were constructed over a period of ten years from 1942 until 1952. Both Darlington and Gorton Works built examples but the largest number, 290, were constructed by the NBL in Glasgow with the Vulcan Foundry also producing fifty engines. *(C.J.B. Sanderson/ARPT)*

Wednesday 25 July 1956. Seen here at the head of an Up TPO near Stonehaven is BR Standard Class 6P5F 4–6–2 no. 72009 *Clan Stewart*. Built at Crewe Works early in 1952 she was allocated to Carlisle Kingmoor shed and could be found working anywhere between Aberdeen and Manchester. She was withdrawn during August 1965. Note that the first three carriages in the train are TPO vehicles, which after the end of every journey would have to be turned for the return trip. This was either carried out on a convenient triangle, or in the case of Aberdeen, they would be turned on the turntable at Kittybrewster shed. *(R. Butterfield/Initial Photographics)*

August 1956. The 'Glens' were the second of the W.P. Reid superheated 4–4–0s and designed specifically for work on the West Highland line and its extension to Mallaig. Constructed between 1913 and 1920, the bulk of the thirty-two class members became associated with that route. During the early 1950s eight members of the class were sent north to assist with workings on the ex-GNoSR section of British Railways. Here we see no. 62493 *Glen Gloy* simmering in the yard at Kittybrewster shed in Aberdeen. Built at Cowlairs Works in 1920, she would be withdrawn during June 1960. *(C.J.B. Sanderson/ARPT)*

Friday 3 August 1956. The roundhouse at Inverness was entered through this magnificent Doric-style archway, the top of which was utilised as water storage tanks. Ex-LMS Class 5 4–6–0 no. 45366 sits on one of the outside roads adjacent to the archway. Constructed by Armstrong Whitworth & Co. during 1937 she would be withdrawn from service in April 1964. The shed was closed to steam locomotives in April 1962 and the archway would be demolished along with the rest of the roundhouse in 1963. *(F.W. Hampson/ARPT)*

Thursday 16 August 1956. Working a Keith to Aviemore service via the Speyside line, ex-CR Class 812 (LMS Class 3F) 0–6–0 no. 57591 is seen at the Cromdale stop. Built by Sharp Stewart & Co. for the CR during 1900, this locomotive would see sixty-one years of service before being withdrawn in June 1961. The Speyside line between Craigellachie and Aviemore was opened in August 1866 and traversed some of the most beautiful countryside in Scotland. Apart from the seasonal shooting and fishing traffic, a major contributor to the goods service on the line was the number of distilleries that it served with grain and malt incoming and bulk whisky outgoing to the blenders and bottlers in the south. From November 1958, passenger services were handled by lightweight diesel railbuses but these did not save the service which closed during October 1968, goods services being withdrawn between November 1968 and November 1971. *(W.S. Sellar)*

Friday 17 August 1956. Seen here in the yard at Inverurie Works after an overhaul and with a slight feather of steam at the safety valve, is ex-NBR Class A (LNER Class N15) 0–6–2 tank no. 69136. Constructed by the NBL and entering service during 1910, she would be withdrawn in May 1961. *(H.D. Ramsey/Initial Photographics)*

Friday 19 April 1957. At Craiglockhart station on the Edinburgh suburban 'Inner Circle', ex-LNER Class K4 2–6–0 no. 61994 *The Great Marquess* is seen working a goods train from Cadder yard in Glasgow to Niddrie. Designed by Nigel Gresley specifically for work on the West Highland line and its extension to Mallaig, the five locomotives of the class were constructed at Darlington Works between January 1937 and January 1939 with this example entering service during July 1938. Based at Eastfield shed in Glasgow for the bulk of its working life, it ended its days at Thornton shed where it would be withdrawn in December 1961. Fortunately it was purchased privately and is once again working on main line specials. *(W.S. Sellar)*

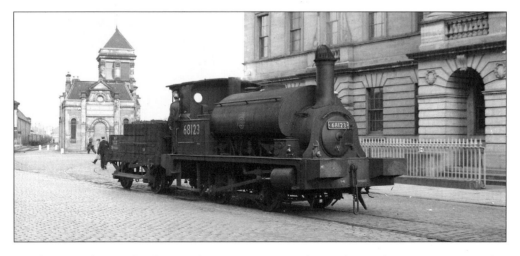

Monday 22 April 1957. This photograph epitomises street working with steam locomotives. Ex-NBR Class G (LNER Class Y9) 0–4–0 saddle tank no. 68123, coupled to a wooden coal tender, is proceeding along Dock Street in Dundee to reach the docks. Fitted with a rudimentary spark arrester this locomotive was built at Cowlairs Works in 1899 based on an original design by Neilson & Co. She would survive a further three years after this photograph was taken, to be withdrawn during August 1960. The building on the right is the Customs House which is now Category A listed. The scene and buildings in the background were completely swept away when the Tay Road Bridge was constructed. *(W.S. Sellar)*

Monday 22 April 1957. Waiting to depart Dundee Tay Bridge shed is ex-NBR Class L (LNER Class C16) 4–4–2 tank no. 67491. A well-balanced and good-looking class of locomotive, this one was built by the NBL in 1916 and was withdrawn during March 1960. *(W.S. Sellar)*

Wednesday 24 April 1957. Hurrying toward Morningside Road station on the Edinburgh suburban 'Outer Circle' is ex-LNER Class V1 2-6-2 tank no. 67649. This locomotive was a product of Doncaster Works during December 1935 and was allocated new to St Margarets shed in Edinburgh, spending her entire working life based there from where she was withdrawn in July 1962. This example was a member of the class never to be rebuilt as a V3. The coaching stock is the classic Edinburgh suburban rake comprising two articulated twins with a single coach marshalled between them. *(W.S. Sellar)*

Saturday 8 June 1957. Ex-GNR Class H3 (LNER Class K2) 2–6–0 no. 61791 *Loch Laggan* is seen here at Fort William shed. Built by Kitson & Co. in 1921 she would be allocated to Eastfield shed in Glasgow during the mid-1920s and was withdrawn from service in March 1960. *(F.W. Hampson/ARPT)*

Sunday 9 June 1957. Ex-NBR Class L (LNER Class C16) 4–4–2 tank no. 67486 is out of steam and undergoing some maintenance inside Dundee West shed. Built by the NBL in 1915 she would give forty-five years of service before being withdrawn in April 1960. Note the solid-looking wooden roof structure of the shed supported on cast iron columns. *(F.W. Hampson/ARPT)*

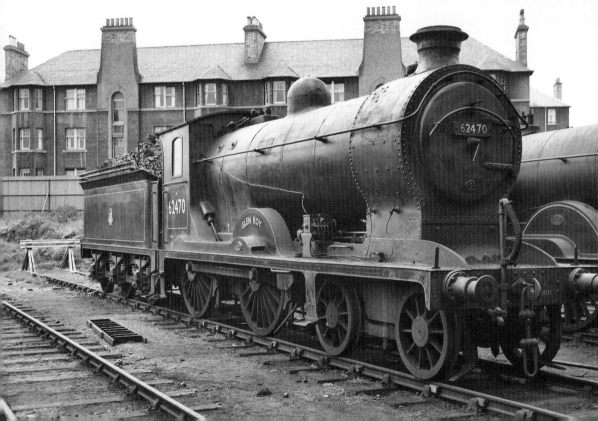

Sunday 23 June 1957. Ex-NBR Class B (LNER Class J37) 0–6–0 no. 64547 is seen here at Inverurie Works having just completed an overhaul. Constructed at Cowlairs Works as a superheated locomotive during 1915 she was, at the time of this photograph, allocated to St Margarets shed in Edinburgh. She would be one of the last of the class to be withdrawn from service in December 1966. The works at Inverurie were closed during December 1969. *(C.J.B. Sanderson/ARPT)*

Opposite, top: **Sunday 9 June 1957**. This well cared for locomotive is the resident St Rollox Works shunter. Ex-CR Class 264 (LMS 0F) 0–4–0 saddle tank no. 56025 has been outshopped in full lined black livery and carries conventional buffers fitted over her dumb buffers. Built at the same works in 1890 she would have a working life of over seventy years before being withdrawn in May 1960. One of thirty-four examples that constituted the class, they were built over a period of twenty-three years from 1885 until 1908. *(F.W. Hampson/ARPT)*

Opposite, bottom: **Sunday 9 June 1957**. Ex-NBR Class K 'Glen' (LNER Class D34) 4–4–0 no. 62470 *Glen Roy* sits at the back of Perth shed. This successful class numbered thirty-two locomotives all constructed at Cowlairs Works between 1913 and 1920. This example entered service in 1913 and would be withdrawn during May 1959. *(F.W. Hampson/ARPT)*

Wednesday 31 July 1957. Preparing to depart from Aberfeldy station with a two-coach branch working to Ballinluig is ex-CR Class 439 (LMS Class 2P) 0–4–4 tank no. 55226. Built at St Rollox Works in 1914 she would be withdrawn from service during September 1961. Note the milk churns and the 'Lyons Cakes' boxes being loaded onto the coach. The branch was opened by the Highland Railway in July 1865 and survived almost 100 years, closing in May 1965. *(A.G. Forsyth/Initial Photographics)*

Tuesday 6 August 1957. Seen standing in the yard at her home shed, 66C Hamilton, is BR Standard Class 3MT 2–6–0 no. 77006. One of a class of only twenty and built at Swindon Works during 1954, she looks in good condition and remained based at Hamilton until reallocated to Motherwell shed in the early 1960s. She would be withdrawn in March 1966. *(A.G. Forsyth/Initial Photographics)*

Tuesday 6 August 1957. Seen here running round the branch train at Killin Junction is ex-CR Class 439 (LMS Class 2P) 0–4–4 tank no. 55222. A product of St Rollox Works in 1914 she would be withdrawn during September 1961. *(W.S. Sellar)*

Tuesday 6 August 1957. This excellent photograph shows ex-LMS Class 5 4–6–0 no. 45099 at the head of an Oban to Glasgow Buchanan Street service having just passed the recently removed site of St Brides crossing in the Pass of Leny. This section of the Callander and Oban Railway route was suddenly closed to all traffic after a landslide in Glenogle on 27 September 1965. The line between Crianlarich (Lower) and Callander was lifted soon afterwards. Glasgow to Oban trains were diverted by the West Highland line to Crianlarich where a connecting spur allowed access to the Oban line. This locomotive was one of the early examples of the class built by the Vulcan Foundry during 1935; she would be withdrawn in September 1963. *(W.S. Sellar)*

Saturday 10 August 1957. This scene at Craigendoran station shows ex-NBR Class M (LNER Class C15) 4–4–2 tank no. 67474 taking water before her next journey. Known by the crews as 'Yorkies' due the manufacturer of the class being the Yorkshire Engine Co., this example entered service in 1913, was fitted for push-pull working during 1954 and saw service on the Craigendorran to Arrochar services until replaced by DMUs in early 1960. She would be withdrawn during April of that year. The pier in the background was opened during 1882 to serve the increasing amount of steamer traffic plying in the Firth of Clyde and still saw rail traffic, which even at the time of this photograph included fuel tank wagons. The last steamer service called at the pier during 1972 and since then it has slowly deteriorated through the actions of time and tide. *(H.D. Ramsey/Initial Photographics)*

Monday 16 September 1957. Sitting in a line of locomotives at Hawick shed is ex-NBR Class J 'Superheated Scott' (LNER Class D30) 4–4–0 no. 62425 *Ellangowan*, an example of the class constructed at Cowlairs Works during 1914 that would be withdrawn in July 1958. She is named after the fictional castle at the centre of Sir Walter Scott's 1815 novel *Guy Mannering*. *(C.J.B. Sanderson/ARPT)*

Thursday 26 September 1957. Drumochter (Druimuachdar) summit is, at approximately 1,500ft above sea level, the highest main line railway in Britain. With a 17-mile climb in the Down direction starting at Blair Atholl, in steam days the heaviest trains were either double-headed or given banking assistance. Seen here approaching the summit at the head of a train mostly comprising of coal wagons is a very leaky ex-LMS Class 5 4–6–0 no. 44980. The fireman, leaning out of the cab window, has obviously done a good job as there is a feather of steam at the safety valves although there are serious leaks from the piston valves and the injector clacks on the top of the boiler. Built at Crewe Works in 1946 she would be withdrawn during July 1965. *(B.W.L. Brooksbank/Initial Photographics)*

Thursday 26 September 1957. In contrast to the previous photograph, ex-LMS Class 5 4–6–0 no. 45475 appears to be perfectly steam tight as she breasts the summit of the climb at Drumochter with a Perth to Inverness service. A product of Derby Works from 1943, she would be withdrawn from service in September 1966. *(B.W.L. Brooksbank/Initial Photographics)*

Saturday 8 February 1958. This winter scene at Galashiels sees ex-NBR Class C (LNER Class J36) 0–6–0 no. 65327 taking time off between snow-clearing duties. Designed by Matthew Holmes and introduced during 1888, many of the class survived to work well into the 1960s, several giving more than sixty years' service. The locomotive seen here was constructed at Cowlairs Works in 1900 and she would be withdrawn during November 1965. *(W.S. Sellar)*

Opposite, top: **Wednesday 12 March 1958**. The Edinburgh Suburban and South Side Junction Railway was opened to passenger traffic during December 1884. Newington station was positioned on a rather cramped site and subsequently was the only station on the line with an island platform. On this wintry day ex-LNER Class V3 2–6–2 tank no. 67668 enters the station with an 'Inner Circle' service. Built at Doncaster Works during 1938 she was constructed as a Class V1 and was converted to Class V3 in 1954, before being withdrawn in December 1962. The suburban service was turned over to DMUs during June 1958 and the passenger service would be withdrawn during September 1962. *(W.S. Sellar)*

Opposite, bottom: **Tuesday 1 April 1958**. Ex-NBR Class J 'Superheated Scott' (LNER Class D30) 4–4–0 no. 62422 *Caleb Balderstone* is seen here in the yard at Hawick shed. Buffered up behind her is ex-NBR Class C (LNER Class J36) 0–6–0 no. 65331. *(W.S. Sellar)*

Saturday 21 June 1958. Ex-LNER Class V3 2–6–2 tank no. 67624 is seen here at Gullane station working a Sunday School Special. Built at Doncaster Works during 1931 as a class V1 locomotive, she would be converted to a class V3 during November 1952. Based at St Margarets shed in Edinburgh for her entire working life she would be withdrawn in September 1960. The branch to Gullane was opened during April 1898 but lost its passenger services as early as September 1932. Goods traffic, however, continued until final closure in June 1964. *(W.S. Sellar)*

Opposite, top: **Thursday 10 April 1958**. Ex-NBR Class L (LNER Class C16) 4–4–2 tank no. 67494 is waiting to access the shed road at Grangemouth. Constructed by the NBL and entering service during 1916 this locomotive was allocated new to St Margarets shed in Edinburgh and spent the bulk of her working life there. She would be withdrawn in February 1961 having given almost forty-five years' service. *(W.S. Sellar)*

Opposite, bottom: **Saturday 12 April 1958**. This photograph, taken at St Margarets shed in Edinburgh, shows the family resemblance of two W.P. Reid-designed and superheated 4–4–0 classes. On the left is the earlier ex-NBR Class J 'Superheated Scott' (LNER Class D30) no. 62421 *Laird o' Monkbarns* with 6ft 6in driving wheels. Constructed at Cowlairs Works in 1914 and named after a character from Sir Walter Scott's 1816 novel *The Antiquary*, she would be one of the last pair of the class to be withdrawn, in June 1960. On the right is an example of the better-known ex-NBR Class K (LNER Class D34) commonly known as 'Glens'. With 6ft driving wheels no. 62490 *Glen Fintaig* is still carrying a small snowplough. Built at Cowlairs Works during 1920 she would be withdrawn from service in February 1959. *(W.S. Sellar)*

Saturday 28 June 1958. Bearing a 64A St Margarets shed code, ex-LNER Class D49 4–4–0 no. 62721 *Warwickshire* waits for its next duty in the yard at Perth shed. Constructed at Darlington Works in 1928 and transferred to the Scottish area during the early 1940s, she would be withdrawn two months after this photograph in August 1958. *(C.J.B. Sanderson/ARPT)*

Monday 21 July 1958. This grimy-looking Pug no. 56038, sheltered only partly from the pouring rain at Inverness roundhouse, was the final example of the ex-CR Class 264 (LMS Class 0F) 0–4–0 saddle tank locomotives to be constructed, coming out of St Rollox Works late in 1908. Based on a Dugald Drummond design of 1885 the class consisted of thirty-four locomotives, fourteen of which survived to be incorporated into British Railways stock. This example would be withdrawn during May 1959. *(A. Brown)*

Monday 21 July 1958. The ex-Highland Railway locomotive works at Lochgorm were adjacent to the station at Inverness and were still being used for the maintenance of steam locomotives. This view of the interior of the erection shop shows three 'Black 5's receiving attention; no. 45359 is heading the queue with nos 45478 and 44959 behind. Opened by the Highland Railway in the early 1860s, the works would build less than forty locomotives for that company during its entire working life. *(A. Brown)*

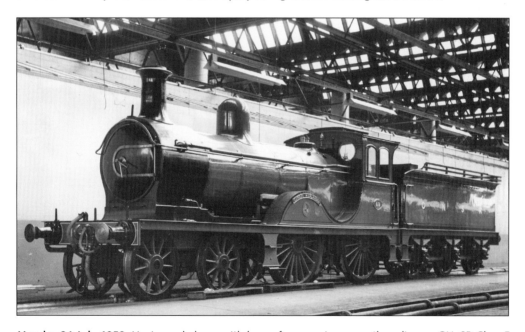

Monday 21 July 1958. Having only been withdrawn from service a month earlier, ex-GNoSR Class F (LNER Class D40) 4–4–0 no. 62277 *Gordon Highlander* is seen here standing in the paint shop at Inverurie Works after completion of a repaint into GNoSR livery. This graceful-looking locomotive was designed by T.E. Heywood and constructed by the NBL as part of a batch of six superheated examples delivered during 1920. Also given her original GNoSR number, 49, she continued working on regular passenger traffic, particularly on the Speyside line, and special trains until June 1966 when she was finally withdrawn from traffic and placed as an exhibit in the Glasgow Museum of Transport. *(A. Brown)*

Tuesday 22 July 1958. This atmospheric photograph shows ex-CR Pickersgill-designed Class 72 (LMS Class 3P) 4–4–0 no. 54488 standing outside Aviemore shed. Built by Armstrong Whitworth & Co. and entering service during 1921, she would be withdrawn forty years later in February 1961. The shed building seen here is still in use today as part of the running shed and works for the Strathspey Railway. *(A. Brown)*

Wednesday 23 July 1958. Seen here stored out of use at Dunfermline shed is ex-NBR Class G (LNER Class Y9) 0–4–0 saddle tank no. 68101. Built at Cowlairs Works during 1889 she would find further use in local yards before being finally withdrawn in October 1962. *(A. Brown)*

Wednesday 23 July 1958. Parked over an inspection pit at Thornton shed is ex-NBR Class K 'Glen' (LNER Class D34) 4–4–0 no. 62468 *Glen Orchy*. The second example of the class to be built at Cowlairs Works in 1913, it would be withdrawn from traffic only two months after this photograph was taken. *(A. Brown)*

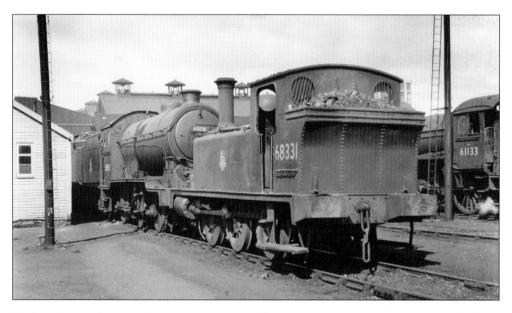

Wednesday 23 July 1958. Sitting among a group of much larger locomotives at Thornton shed, and looking diminutive by comparison, is ex-NBR Class F (LNER Class J88) 0–6–0 tank no. 68331. Built at Cowlairs Works in 1905 this locomotive would serve for fifty-four years before being withdrawn during March 1959. Fitted with dumb buffers to accommodate shunting in tight radius yards, this example was based at Kipps shed in Glasgow for many years before ending her days at Thornton. *(A. Brown)*

Saturday 8 November 1958. Seen here at St Leonards yard in Edinburgh is a locomotive that performed the same duty of St Leonards pilot throughout its entire working life. Ex-NBR Class F (LNER Class J88) 0–6–0 tank no. 68338 was allocated new to St Margarets shed after construction at Cowlairs Works in 1912. She gave forty-nine years' service before being withdrawn during September 1961. *(W.S. Sellar)*

Opposite, top: **Wednesday 8 October 1958**. Utilised on the suburban services between Dundee East and Arbroath, ex-NBR Class L (LNER Class C16) 4–4–2 tank no. 67502 is waiting for its next duty at Arbroath. The last of the class of twenty-one to be built by the NBL, she entered service during March 1921 and would be withdrawn in April 1960. Allocated new to the Glasgow area to work suburban traffic around that city, she would end her working life based at Dundee. The seven stations between Dundee East and Arbroath were well catered for by this service with fourteen trains each way per weekday. *(W.S. Sellar)*

Opposite, bottom: **Thursday 9 October 1958**. Waiting to depart Elgin GNoSR station is the branch train to Lossiemouth headed by ex-CR Class 439 (LMS Class 2P) 0–4–4 tank no. 55221 looking in good, clean condition. Built at St Rollox Works in 1914 she would be withdrawn during October 1961. The Lossiemouth branch was opened in August 1852 and at one time saw a dozen trains each way per weekday; however, by 1958 it was poorly served with a sparse three trains each way per weekdays – one morning, one mid-day and one evening. Fish traffic constituted the main reason for the branch remaining open with passenger services ceasing in April 1964. The goods service closed in March 1966. *(W.S. Sellar)*

Wednesday 25 February 1959. Port Edgar lay on the south side of the River Forth and was home to the HM Mine Warfare depot – HMS *Lochinvar*. The South Queensferry branch served the yard at Port Edgar with a daily goods and on this day we see ex-NBR Class C (LNER Class J36) 0–6–0 no. 65243 between duties in the yard. This locomotive was also known as *Maude* but at this time she was not carrying the name which would be restored to her during 1960. Port Edgar had been used during the First World War as a base for torpedo boats with HMS *Lochinvar* being established there during 1939 as a base for minesweepers and minelaying vessels. It would be closed during 1975 when activities moved across the River Forth to Rosyth Naval Base. The port is now a busy marina for pleasure craft. *(W.S. Sellar)*

Friday 27 March 1959. Smeaton station and its yard were at the heart of the Lothians coalfield and saw much traffic to and from the pits in the area, particularly that at Dalkeith, in addition to the agricultural traffic coming off the Macmerry and Gifford branches. Ex-NBR Class B (LNER Class J37) 0–6–0 no. 64554 is seen here lifting a long train of empty wagons away from the yard. A June 1916 product of Cowlairs Works, this locomotive would be withdrawn in January 1964. The branches from Smeaton to Macmerry and Gifford were opened during July 1872 and October 1901 respectively, but passenger services were short-lived with the Macmerry branch losing its service in July 1925 and Gifford losing its in April 1933. Goods services continued to Macmerry until May 1960 and to Gifford until May 1965. *(W.S. Sellar)*

Friday 3 April 1959. The stone-built locomotive shed seen here is at St Boswells and it was sited conveniently next to the station. Ex-NBR Class B (LNER Class J35) 0–6–0 no. 64494 has been parked outside the shed while the driver and his mate have a conversation. This example of the class was constructed by the NBL and entered service during November 1909. She would be rebuilt with a superheated boiler during 1926 and was withdrawn in June 1961 having given fifty-two years of service. St Boswells was the sub-shed of Hawick that supplied locomotives for the branches to Jedburgh, the Tweed Valley line to Berwick and the old NBR line to Reston. The coaching stock for the Tweed Valley line service can be seen in the bay platform. *(A. Brown)*

Friday 3 April 1959. Kelso signal-box stands prominently above this local train from St Boswells to Coldstream and Berwick. The locomotive in charge is ex-LNER Class V3 2–6–2 tank no. 67606, built at Doncaster Works in 1939 as a class V1 – she would be converted to a class V3 during 1952. Allocated new to St Margarets shed in Edinburgh, she spent all her working life in the area and would be withdrawn in December 1962. The Tweed Valley line to Kelso, from its junction at St Boswells, opened to traffic during June 1851 and served the important market towns of Kelso and Coldstream on its route to Tweedmouth where it joined the East Coast Main Line. Passenger trains ceased in June 1964 with goods traffic finally being withdrawn from Kelso in April 1968. *(A. Brown)*

Saturday 9 May 1959. Working hard while banking the goods train seen in the photograph (opposite, bottom) is ex-NBR Class C (LNER Class J36) 0–6–0 no. 65224 *Mons*. Constructed at Cowlairs Works in 1891 this locomotive was one of twenty-five of the class to serve in France with the R.O.D. during the First World War. She would be rebuilt in the form we see here during 1915 and went on to be one of the longest-working members of the class, finally being withdrawn in May 1963 after seventy-two years. *(W.S. Sellar)*

Opposite, top: **Saturday 4 April 1959**. This day saw the Branch Line Society's 'The Scott Country Railtour' visiting Galashiels, Selkirk, Roxburgh, Jedburgh and St Boswells. Motive power was St Margarets' long-time resident ex-NBR Class K (LNER Class D34) 4–4–0 no. 62471 *Glen Falloch*. Bearing a 64A shed code and looking very smart, she is seen here at Galashiels station. Built at Cowlairs Works in 1913 this locomotive would be withdrawn after forty-seven years of service during March 1960. The trackbed and station site in this photograph are now occupied by a town centre bypass road. *(W.S. Sellar)*

Opposite, bottom: **Saturday 9 May 1959**. Working a southbound goods train near Fushiebridge on the 1 in 70 climb to Fallahill is ex-GNR Class H4 (LNER Class K3) 2–6–0 no. 61858. Built at Darlington Works during 1925, she was allocated new to Carlisle Canal shed and appears to have spent her entire working life based there – she is still bearing a 12C shed code and the shed name is painted on the front buffer beam. These Nigel Gresley-designed three-cylinder locomotives first appeared during 1920 for the Great Northern Railway and so successful were they that construction continued until 1937 with a total of 193 examples being produced. The example seen here would be withdrawn during April 1961. *(W.S. Sellar)*

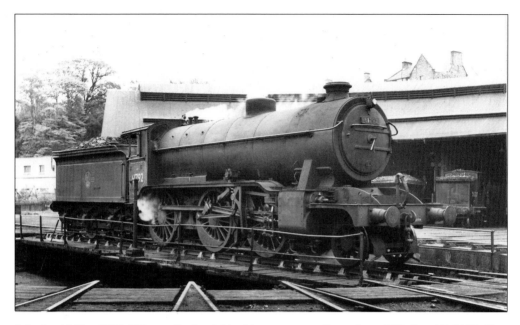

Saturday 16 May 1959. Sitting on the turntable at Inverness roundhouse is ex-GNR Class H3 (LNER Class K2) 2–6–0 no. 61792. One of Nigel Gresley's early designs for the GNR, these two-cylinder locomotives proved very successful with many examples being allocated to Scottish sheds during LNER days, a number being named after lochs in the west of Scotland. This example was constructed by Kitson & Co. 1921, transferred to Kittybrewster shed in 1952, and was withdrawn in September 1960. *(R.J. Buckley/Initial Photographics)*

Saturday 16 May 1959. Simmering outside Keith shed is ex-GNR Class H3 (LNER Class K2) 2–6–0 no. 61755. One of the NBL constructed members of the class delivered in 1918, she would be withdrawn from service only six months after this photograph was taken, in November 1959. *(R.J. Buckley/Initial Photographics)*

Saturday 16 May 1959. This ex-CR Pickersgill-designed Class 113 (LMS Class 3P) 4–4–0 no. 54471 is only months away from being withdrawn – this took place in October of the same year. Built by the NBL during 1916 it is seen here at Forres shed. *(R.J. Buckley/Initial Photographics)*

Sunday 17 May 1959. Standing within a line of locomotives at Perth shed is ex-LNER Class V2 2–6–2 no. 60834. One of the Darlington Works-built examples, she entered traffic during September 1938 and was allocated new to Ferryhill shed in Aberdeen. It would be 1961 before any members of this highly successful class would be withdrawn, no. 60834 ending her service in March 1964. The last two class members went to the scrapyard during December 1966. *(R.J. Buckley/Initial Photographics)*

Sunday 17 May 1959. Sitting in the yard at Grangemouth shed is ex-Ministry of Supply Class WD 8F 2–10–0 no. 90766. Bearing a 65F Grangemouth shed code, this locomotive was built by the NBL during 1945 and numbered 73790 by the War Department. The NBL built a total of 150 of these locomotives between 1943 and 1945, most of which were destined to see service in Europe towards the end of the Second World War. Many remained in Europe after the war, particularly those in Holland and four examples of the class have been preserved, three in the UK and one in Holland. Purchased by British Railways during 1948 and initially allocated to Motherwell shed, no. 90766 would end her days working out of Grangemouth from where she would be withdrawn in December 1962. *(R.J. Buckley/Initial Photographics)*

Sunday 17 May 1959. A veteran of 1883, this ex-CR Class 294 (LMS Class 2F) 0–6–0 no. 57232 was designed by Dugald Drummond as one of thirty-five built by Neilson & Co. Destined to work for seventy-eight years, she was withdrawn from service in May 1961, and she is seen here sporting a stovepipe chimney in the yard at Perth shed. A total of 163 examples of the class were built over a period of twelve years, the greater majority by the Caley themselves at St Rollox Works. *(R.J. Buckley/Initial Photographics)*

Monday 18 May 1959. Clean WDs were something of a rarity, so this photograph of Class 8F 2–10–0 no. 90761 at Eastfield shed in Glasgow makes a fine impression. Built by the NBL during 1945 and allocated the number 73785 by the WD, she would be one of a batch of twenty-five examples of the class purchased by British Railways during 1948. Allocated to Motherwell shed she would be withdrawn in November 1962. *(R.J. Buckley/Initial Photographics)*

Monday 18 May 1959. BR Standard Class 4MT 2–6–4 tank no. 80026 is looking particularly smart at its home shed, 66A Polmadie. An example of the 1951 Brighton Works-built members of the class, she would be withdrawn during September 1966. A total of 155 examples were constructed by Derby, Brighton and Doncaster Works between 1951 and 1957. *(R.J. Buckley/Initial Photographics)*

Tuesday 21 July 1959. Waiting to depart from Stirling station with an express to Glasgow is BR Standard Class 5MT 4–6–0 no. 73009. Delivered new to Perth shed from Derby Works in 1951, she was withdrawn in July 1966. *(A. Brown)*

Opposite, top: **Monday 18 May 1959**. At Corkerhill shed in Glasgow, BR Standard Class 4MT 2–6–0 no. 76092 waits to leave the shed for its next duty. Built at Horwich Works in 1957 she would be withdrawn during August 1966 having given only ten years' service. A total of 115 members of the class were constructed at Horwich and Doncaster Works between 1952 and 1957. *(R.J. Buckley/Initial Photographics)*

Opposite, bottom: **Saturday 23 May 1959**. Approaching Fushiebridge station with a passenger service from Edinburgh to Carlisle is ex-LNER Class B1 4–6–0 no. 61025 *Pallah*. One of the Darlington-built examples of the class, she entered service during April 1947 and would be withdrawn in December 1962. *(W.S. Sellar)*

Wednesday 22 July 1959. Waiting to depart from Oban station with a passenger train to Ballachulish is ex-CR Class 439 (LMS Class 2P) 0–4–4 tank no. 55230. A 1915 product of St Rollox Works, she would be withdrawn during September 1961. *(A. Brown)*

Thursday 23 July 1959. This general view of Fort William shed has two of the ex-LNER Class K locomotives parked in the yard. On the left is K1/1 2–6–0 no. 61997 *MacCailin Mor* which was originally constructed at Darlington Works in 1938/9 as a Nigel Gresley-designed three-cylinder Class K4 locomotive, destined for use on the West Highland line. During 1945, Gresley's successor, Edward Thompson, arranged for the planned rebuilding of the K4s into two-cylinder locomotives but only one was completed – LNER no. 3445 (BR no. 61997). She would eventually be allocated to Fort William from where she was withdrawn during June 1961. The locomotive standing ahead of 61997 is ex-GNR Class H3 (LNER Class K2) no. 61794 *Loch Oich*. A Nigel Gresley design of 1912, this locomotive was built by Kitson & Co. The last of the class to enter service during September 1921, she was withdrawn in July 1960. *(A. Brown)*

Wednesday 19 August 1959. Being prepared for duty at Eastfield shed in Glasgow is ex-LNER Class J39 0–6–0 no. 64919. Bearing a 56F Low Moor (Bradford) shed code but with Sunderland painted on her front buffer beam, she has probably just exited Cowlairs Works after an overhaul. One of a class of almost 300, they were only rarely allocated to Scottish sheds. Built by Beyer Peacock & Co. during 1936 she would be withdrawn in December 1962. *(D. Dippie/ARPT)*

Wednesday 23 September 1959. The most northerly railway station in the British Isles is at Thurso and it is here that ex-CR Pickersgill Class 72 (LMS Class 3P) 4–4–0 no. 54491 is seen waiting for the loading of wagons to be completed prior to departing with the branch train to Georgemas Junction. Constructed by Armstrong Whitworth & Co. in 1921 she would be withdrawn from service during December 1961. *(W.S. Sellar)*

Friday 2 October 1959. Seen here at Bogside in Fife working the 'Edinburgh and Lothians Miniature Railway Club Charter' is the iconic Caley Single no. 123. Built by Neilson & Co. for the Edinburgh International Exhibition of 1886 it was later purchased by the Caledonian Railway and used by them during the 1888 'Races to the North' working between Carlisle and Edinburgh. Withdrawn from service by the LMS in 1935 and placed on static display, it was brought back into service by British Railways in the early 1960s and used on special workings and railtours. It is currently to be seen at the Glasgow Museum of Transport. *(W.S. Sellar)*

Thursday 21 April 1960. Ex-NBR Class B (LNER Class J35) 0–6–0 no. 64479 has completed the task of shunting in Dalkeith goods yard and is seen here crossing Glenesk Junction on its return to Hardengreen with its train. Built at Cowlairs Works in 1908 this example would be rebuilt with a superheated boiler during 1938 and would be withdrawn from service in December 1961. *(W.S. Sellar)*

Thursday 21 April 1960. The isolated Benhar level crossing signal-box is high up on Fauldhouse Moor which lies between Shotts and Bathgate. A web of lines which one time belonged to the NBR and the CR spread out across the countryside to provide access to many small collieries in the area, a number of which survived into the early 1960s. Seen here standing opposite the signal-box is ex-NBR Class B (LNER Class J35) 0–6–0 no. 64504 waiting to work a goods train to Westcraigs Junction. Constructed by the NBL during 1910 she would be rebuilt with a superheated boiler in 1933 and be withdrawn five months after this photograph was taken during September 1960. *(W.S. Sellar)*

Saturday 23 April 1960. Ex-LNER Class A3 4–6–2 no. 60043 *Brown Jack* was the last of the class to be constructed at Doncaster Works in 1935 and named after the racehorse that won the Queen Alexandra Stakes between 1929 and 1934. Seen here departing from Galashiels station at the head of a stopper from Edinburgh to Carlisle, she had by this time acquired a double chimney but has yet to be equipped with smoke deflectors. Allocated new to Haymarket shed she would finally be based at St Margarets in Edinburgh before withdrawal during May 1964. *(W.S. Sellar)*

Saturday 14 May 1960. Restarting from under the large signal gantry at the south end of Carstairs station is Motherwell-allocated ex-LMS Class 5 4–6–0 no. 45484 with an early morning Up goods train for the Carlisle line. Built at Derby Works in 1943 she would be withdrawn during February 1964. *(Michael Mensing)*

Saturday 14 May 1960. With appropriate lamp head code, ex-LMS Class 5 4–6–0 no. 45443, bearing a St Rollox shed code, waits to depart from Glasgow Buchanan Street station with the 12.00 noon departure to Oban. A 1937 product of Armstrong Whitworth & Co., she would be withdrawn in August 1965. Buchanan Street station was closed in November 1966 with services being transferred to Queen Street station. St Rollox shed which supplied motive power for services from Buchanan Street was closed during the same month. *(Michael Mensing)*

Monday 16 May 1960. Seen entering Killin Junction station at the head of a four-coach stopper from Glasgow Buchanan Street to Oban is ex-LMS Class 5 4–6–0 no. 44880. Built at Crewe Works in 1945, she would be withdrawn from service during November 1966. *(Michael Mensing)*

Tuesday 17 May 1960. At Taynuilt station a Down goods train, consisting of Presflo Alumina wagons from Burntisland, is seen arriving behind ex-LMS Class 5 4–6–0 no. 45214 with its driver preparing to hand over the pouch containing the single line section token to the signalman. One of the early 1935-built examples by Armstrong Whitworth & Co., she would serve for thirty-one years before being withdrawn in December 1966. *(Michael Mensing)*

Thursday 19 May 1960. Ex-LMS Class 5 4–6–0 no. 45443 is waiting to be joined by a pilot locomotive before departing with the 5.15 p.m. service to Glasgow Buchanan Street and Edinburgh Princes Street. In the background is ex-CR Class 439 (LMS Class 2P) 0–4–4 tank no. 55224 which is waiting to depart with the 4.55 p.m. service to Ballachulish. (Michael Mensing)

Opposite, top: **Tuesday 17 May 1960**. At Taynuilt station again, this time with ex-LMS Class 5 4–6–0 no. 44795, a Carlisle Kingmoor-allocated locomotive, arriving with the 12.00 noon Glasgow Buchanan Street to Oban service. Once again a member of the crew is preparing to hand over the single line token to the waiting signalman. This was a Horwich Works-built example of the class, entering service during 1947 and being withdrawn in July 1967. (Michael Mensing)

Opposite, bottom: **Wednesday 18 May 1960**. At the head of a short mineral train, BR Standard Class 4MT 2–6–0 no. 76001, bearing a 66B Motherwell shed code, is seen approaching Oban having just passed Oban Junction signal-box. Built at Horwich Works late in 1952 she would be withdrawn in August 1966. (Michael Mensing)

Thursday 19 May 1960. Waiting for the right of way at Tyndrum Upper station is ex-LMS Class 5 4–6–0 no. 44957 at the head of a permanent way train. Another Horwich Works-built example of the class entering service during 1946, she would be withdrawn in May 1964. *(Michael Mensing)*

Thursday 19 May 1960. At the head of an evening goods train, ex-LMS Class 5 4–6–0 no. 45016 coasts downhill toward Oban. One of the early Crewe Works-built examples from 1935, she would be withdrawn during July 1966. *(Michael Mensing)*

Friday 20 May 1960. Waiting to depart from Ballachulish station with the 3.57 p.m. service to Oban is ex-CR Class 'Enlarged 439' (LMS Class 2P) 0–4–4 tank no. 55238. Constructed in 1922 at St Rollox Works with heavier buffer beams and larger cylinders, the four examples of this batch of the class were intended for banking duties at Beattock but eventually became dispersed throughout the old Caley system. This example would be withdrawn in September 1961. The athletic fireman is climbing over the roof prior to trimming the coal in the bunker. This branch was opened by the Callander and Oban Railway during August 1903 and would be closed to all traffic in March 1966. The old quarry workings in the background were part of the Laroch slate quarries that produced roofing slates which were despatched throughout the United Kingdom. *(Michael Mensing)*

Saturday 21 May 1960. Trundling off the Connel Ferry bridge at the head of an Up Oban-bound goods train is ex-CR Class 812 (LMS Class 3F) 0–6–0 no. 57571. One of a batch of twenty locomotives constructed by Neilson Reid & Co. during 1899/1900 for the Caledonian, she would be withdrawn from service in April 1962. *(Michael Mensing)*

Tuesday 24 May 1960. This view, east of Connel Ferry station, shows the hills of Benderloch rising in the background and the tower of the parish church of Achnaba just visible in the distance, while ex-LMS Class 5 4–6–0 no. 45157 *The Glasgow Highlander*, a long-serving St Rollox resident, hurries along with the 7.55 a.m. service from Glasgow Buchanan Street to Oban. Constructed by Armstrong Whitworth & Co. during 1935, she was withdrawn in December 1962. *(Michael Mensing)*

Tuesday 24 May 1960. This wonderfully scenic photograph with the Connel Ferry Bridge in the background, shows ex-LMS Class 5 4–6–0 no. 45049 at the head of an Oban-bound goods train on the approach to Connel Ferry station. Built at the Vulcan Foundry during 1934 she would be withdrawn in August 1963. The spectacular bridge at Connel Ferry, spanning the narrows at the entrance to Loch Etive, came into use with the opening of the Ballachulish branch in August 1903. It would remain in service until the final branch closure during March 1966, after which it would become a dedicated road bridge. *(Michael Mensing)*

Tuesday 24 May 1960. To the east of Connel Ferry, ex-LMS Class 5 4–6–0 no. 45482 is drifting towards Oban with the 12.00 noon departure from Glasgow Buchanan Street. Built at Derby Works during 1943 she would be withdrawn in June 1964. *(Michael Mensing)*

Tuesday 24 May 1960. A crew member on ex-CR Class 439 (LMS Class 2P) 0–4–4 tank no. 55224 prepares to hand over the section token at Connel Ferry West signal-box while arriving with the 3.57 p.m. Ballachulish to Oban service. Built at St Rollox Works during 1914 this locomotive would be withdrawn in October 1961. *(Michael Mensing)*

Wednesday 25 May 1960. Leaving a smokescreen to drift over the town, Class 5 4–6–0 no. 44677 blasts its way out of Oban station at the head of the 12.05 p.m. service to Glasgow Buchanan Street and Edinburgh Princes Street. *(Michael Mensing)*

Friday 22 July 1960. At Appin station the young fireman of ex-CR Class 439 (LMS Class 2P) 0–4–4 tank no. 55173, working the service to Oban, strikes a pose while waiting for the Oban to Ballachulish service, seen in the background, to enter the station. This locomotive was a product of St Rollox Works in 1900 that would be withdrawn during January 1962. *(A. Brown)*

Monday 25 July 1960. Seen here entering Strathcarron station at the head of a goods train for Kyle of Lochalsh is Inverness-allocated ex-LMS Class 5 4–6–0 no. 45360. Built by Armstrong Whitworth & Co. during 1937 she would be withdrawn in September 1965. *(A. Brown)*

Saturday 18 February 1961. Working a short goods train consisting of one wagon and a brake van, ex-NBR Class C (LNER Class J36) 0–6–0 no. 65345 is seen between Kennoway and Montrave goods stations on the goods-only Lochty branch. This locomotive was the penultimate member of the class to be built at Cowlairs Works during 1900 and rebuilt in 1923. She would be one of the last pair of the class to be withdrawn in June 1967. This 15-mile-long branch was opened by the East Fife Central Railway in 1898 to serve the agricultural community of central Fife and it would be closed in 1965. *(W.S. Sellar)*

Friday 21 April 1961. Ex-LNER Class A3 4–6–2 no. 60087 *Blenheim* is seen here approaching Morningside Road station on the Edinburgh suburban 'Outer Circle' with the 12.35 p.m. Niddrie Yard to Craiginches Yard goods. Built at Doncaster Works in 1930 and named after the Derby winner of the same year, she would be allocated to Haymarket shed in 1937 and by October 1963, when she was withdrawn, she would be based at St Margarets shed in Edinburgh. *(W.S. Sellar)*

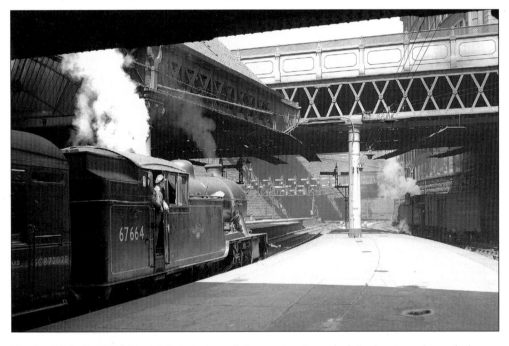

Monday 24 April 1961. This detailed photograph has captured wonderfully the atmosphere of Glasgow Queen Street station during a lull in activity. Ex-LNER Class V1 2–6–2 tank no. 67664 is seen standing at the head of a local to Kirkintilloch, while in the shadows to the right ex-NBR Class A (LNER Class N15) 0–6–2 tank no. 69181 is sitting attached to a couple of vans. The V1 was a product of Doncaster Works during July 1938 which was based at Glasgow sheds for its entire working life. She would be withdrawn in December 1962. The N15 was built by the NBL in February 1917 and would be withdrawn only a few months before the V1, during February 1962. *(W.S. Sellar)*

Saturday 13 May 1961. With the failure of the Glasgow Electric 'Blue Train' EMU stock owing to technical problems in December 1960, steam working of the electrified suburban routes was reintroduced and ran until October 1961 when the electric services recommenced. Class 4MT 2–6–4 tank no. 42057 is seen arriving at Cathcart station with the 8.49 a.m. Uplawmoor to Glasgow Central service. This locomotive was one of the Fairburn variations of an earlier Stanier design. Built at Derby Works in 1950 she would be withdrawn in July 1964. *(Michael Mensing)*

Saturday 13 May 1961. BR Standard Class 4MT 2–6–4 tank no. 80058 is seen departing from Glasgow Central with the 9.30 a.m. service to Gourock. A Derby Works-built example of the class which entered service during 1955, she would survive only eleven years to be withdrawn in July 1966. Note the ex-CR style route indicator in use above the front buffer beam, showing the correct positioning for a Gourock-bound train. *(Michael Mensing)*

Saturday 13 May 1961. This photograph taken from the concourse at Glasgow Queen Street station gives some idea of the immense overall roof spanning the platforms. Class A2 4–6–2 no. 60530 *Sayajirao* has just arrived at platform 3 with a parcels train and is being admired by several groups of people including a boy in full school uniform. Built at Doncaster Works in 1948 she would become the penultimate example of the class to be withdrawn during November 1966 while based at Ferryhill shed in Aberdeen. *(Michael Mensing)*

Monday 15 May 1961. With its single wagon and brake van load, ex-CR Class 652 (LMS Class 3F) 0–6–0 no. 57635 waits at Connel Ferry station before proceeding to Oban. *(Michael Mensing)*

Monday 15 May 1961. Coming off the north end of Connel Ferry Bridge with the 4.55 p.m. Oban to Ballachulish service is veteran ex-CR Class 19 (LMS Class 2P) 0–4–4 tank no. 55124. The last survivor of its class of ten built at St Rollox Works in 1895, it would lead something of a nomadic life being allocated to several Glasgow sheds, Grangemouth, Dumfries and finally to Dalry Road in Edinburgh where it lay for a long period after withdrawal in October 1961. Note the differing outline of the coal bunker compared to later-built examples. *(Michael Mensing)*

Tuesday 16 May 1961. Ex-LMS Class 2P 0–4–4 tank no. 55263 is preparing to move empty stock at Oban station. One of ten locomotives constructed for the LMS by Nasmyth, Wilson & Co. in 1925, the design was a continuation of the Class 439 but had a slightly larger water tank capacity. This engine would be withdrawn in November 1961. *(Michael Mensing)*

Monday 22 May 1961. Bearing a 63B, Fort William shed code, ex-NBR Class C (LNER Class J36) 0–6–0 no. 65313 is seen moving empty stock out of Fort William station. This locomotive was a product of Cowlairs Works during 1899 and would be rebuilt in 1921. In total it survived for sixty-three years before being withdrawn in July 1962. *(Michael Mensing)*

Opposite, top: **Thursday 18 May 1961**. Making a spirited departure from Connel Ferry station with the 7.50 a.m. Glasgow Buchanan Street to Oban service is ex-LMS Class 5 4–6–0 no. 45423. Built by Armstrong Whitworth & Co. during 1937, she would be withdrawn thirty years later in May 1967. *(Michael Mensing)*

Opposite, bottom: **Monday 22 May 1961**. At the head of a goods train destined for Mallaig, A.H. Peppercorn-designed Class K1 2–6–0 no. 62012 is seen passing the barrel yard at the Glenlochy Distillery in Fort William. Built by the NBL during 1949 she would be withdrawn in May 1967. The distillery had its own sidings which can be seen in the background. Since closure the building has been converted to flats and houses have been constructed in the yard. *(Michael Mensing)*

Thursday 25 May 1961. This splendid photograph shows Class K1 2–6–0 no. 62052, bearing a Fort William shed code, departing from Fort William with a service for Glasgow Queen Street. Built by the NBL in 1949 she would be withdrawn during December 1962. *(Michael Mensing)*

Opposite, top: **Tuesday 23 May 1961**. Arriving at Fort William with a goods train is Class 5 4–6–0 no. 44702. Constructed at Horwich Works in 1948 she would be withdrawn in June 1965. *(Michael Mensing)*

Opposite, bottom: **Thursday 25 May 1961**. Seen shunting some vans in the yard at Fort William is ex-LMS Class 4F 0–6–0 no. 44255. A post-grouping development of the Midland Railway Class 4, she was built at Derby Works in 1926 and transferred to Fort William during 1958. She would be withdrawn from service in December 1962. This class was selected as the standard LMS goods locomotive and nearly 600 examples were constructed by Derby, Crewe, St Rollox and Horwich works. Outside contractors were also manufacturing the class with the NBL in Glasgow, Kerr Stuart of Stoke and even Andrew Barclay in Kilmarnock delivering twenty-five examples. Note that the locomotive shown here is paired with a self-weighing tender. *(Michael Mensing)*

Friday 26 May 1961. Class K1 2–6–0 no. 62034 is seen here at Mallaig station reversing onto the coaching stock that will form the 1.00 p.m. service to Glasgow Queen Street. Built by the NBL in 1949 she would be withdrawn during December 1962. In the background can be seen the locomotive shed, behind the rake of cattle wagons. *(Michael Mensing)*

Friday 26 May 1961. Arriving at Fort William station is BR Standard Class 5MT 4–6–0 no. 73078 piloting ex-LMS Class 5 4–6–0 no. 44975 with the 5.45 a.m. departure from Glasgow which incorporates sleeping cars from London King's Cross. The Standard Class 5 was delivered new to Eastfield shed from Derby Works during 1955 and would have a very short working life of only eleven years before being withdrawn in July 1966. The 'Black 5' was constructed at Crewe Works during 1946 and would be withdrawn from service a year before the Standard in September 1965. *(Michael Mensing)*

Saturday 27 May 1961. Ex-LNER Class A3 4–6–2 no. 60082 *Neil Gow* is seen departing from Glasgow St Enoch with the 4.00 p.m. service to Leeds City via Kilmarnock, Dumfries and Carlisle. She was one of the twenty examples of the class constructed by the NBL during 1924 and was named after the famous Scottish fiddle player. She acquired the double chimney in 1959 but had yet to be fitted with smoke deflectors. She would be withdrawn in September 1963. *(Michael Mensing)*

Saturday 27 May 1961. Being admired by three young enthusiasts, BR Standard Class 7P6F 'Britannia' 4–6–2 no. 70050 *Firth of Clyde* is waiting to depart from Glasgow Central with the 4.30 p.m. service to Liverpool Exchange and Manchester Victoria. Built at Crewe Works in 1954 and allocated to Polmadie shed in Glasgow, she would be withdrawn only twelve years later in August 1966. *(Michael Mensing)*

Sunday 2 July 1961. At Princes Street station in Edinburgh, ex-LMS Class 4MT 2–6–4 tank no. 42204, bearing a 66E Carstairs shed code, departs with empty coaching stock for the sidings. A product of Derby Works in 1945 she would be withdrawn during December 1966. *(Author)*

Opposite, top: **Thursday 1 June 1961**. Seen here passing Niddrie South Junction on the outskirts of Edinburgh, is ex-NBR Class C (LNER Class J36) 0–6–0 no. 65327. A veteran of 1900 constructed at Cowlairs Works, she would be rebuilt in the form seen here during 1922 and was withdrawn in November 1965. The long train of empty unfitted mineral wagons she has behind her were from the yard at Portobello and probably destined for the Lady Victoria Colliery at Newtongrange. *(W.S. Sellar)*

Opposite, bottom: **Thursday 29 June 1961**. In beautifully clean condition, a credit to the staff at Haymarket shed, ex-LNER Class A4 4–6–2 no. 60004 *William Whitelaw* is seen about to leave Craigentinny Carriage Sidings with the empty stock for the 5.15 p.m. Edinburgh Waverley to Glasgow Queen Street service. Allocated to Haymarket shed during 1941, she would be transferred to Ferryhill in Aberdeen in 1962 to join some of her classmates in operating the fast three-hour expresses to Glasgow. *(W.S. Sellar)*

Sunday 9 July 1961. The Jedburgh branch opened to traffic in July 1856 from a junction at Roxburgh and passenger services lasted until August 1948 when they were withdrawn after serious flooding in the area. However, goods services continued until August 1964. This day saw the visiting RCTS West Yorkshire Branch 'Borders Railtour' hauled by ex-NBR Class B (LNER Class J37) 0-6-0 no. 64624 and we see her arriving at Jedburgh with the signalman waiting to receive the branch token. Built by the NBL in 1921, she would be withdrawn from service during January 1966. *(W.S. Sellar)*

Friday 28 July 1961. The smoke-filled atmosphere at St Margarets shed is clearly evident here as ex-LNER Class J38 0-6-0 no. 65920 prepares to depart from the yard. Designed by Nigel Gresley specifically to handle heavy goods traffic in Scotland, the thirty-five examples of this powerful class were all constructed at Darlington Works during 1926 and would be classified 6F by British Railways. All were allocated to sheds in Fife, Glasgow, Edinburgh and Dundee and the bulk of the class continued working well into the 1960s with the last two being withdrawn during April 1967. The locomotive shown here was withdrawn in November 1966. *(D. Dippie/ARPT)*

Sunday 31 July 1961. Performing empty coach stock duties and seen here taking water at Glasgow St Enoch station is Class 4MT 2–6–4 tank no. 42190. A 1948 product of Derby Works she would be withdrawn during June 1964. *(D. Dippie/ARPT)*

Saturday 12 August 1961. Mr Wilson, the stationmaster at Duddingston, assists in overseeing the passage of ex-NBR Class B (LNER Cass J35) 0–6–0 no. 64479 while crossing the Duddingston Road West at Cairntows level crossing, with a train of empty mineral wagons from St Leonards yard in Edinburgh. The locomotive is paired with a tender that incorporates a tender cab fitting to give additional protection to the crews during adverse weather. *(W.S. Sellar)*

Tuesday 15 August 1961. BR Standard Class 2MT 2–6–0 no. 78049, bearing a 64C Dalry Road Edinburgh shed code, is waiting to depart from Tweedmouth station with a train for St Boswells via the Tweed Valley line. She has worked into the station with the train from Berwick, on the opposite side of the River Tweed, and has run round prior to departing. The guard is walking along the platform with the headlamp for the loco. Built at Darlington Works during 1955 she would be withdrawn in August 1966. *(A.G. Forsyth/ Initial Photographics)*

Opposite, top: **Tuesday 2 January 1962**. This wintry scene is on the approach to Balquhidder station and with the lower quadrant home in the off position, ex-LMS Class 5 4–6–0 no. 45158 *Glasgow Yeomanry* is seen in charge of an Oban to Glasgow Buchanan Street service. Constructed by Armstrong Whitworth & Co. during 1935, she would be withdrawn in July 1964. *(W.S. Sellar)*

Opposite, bottom: **Tuesday 16 January 1962**. The passenger service on the Wilsontown branch had been withdrawn during September 1951 but goods services continued until May 1964 primarily to serve the Kingshill Colliery at the head of the branch. The daily goods is seen here at Wilsontown station behind ex-CR Class 300 (LMS Class 3F) 0–6–0 no. 57670. A 1918 product of St Rollox Works, she would be withdrawn in March 1963. *(W.S. Sellar)*

Friday 6 April 1962. With a train of mineral wagons behind her, ex-NBR Class B (LNER Class J37) 0–6–0 no. 64626 is seen near Little Mill Colliery high up on the Ayrshire moors. Constructed by the NBL during 1921 she would be withdrawn in November 1963. *(W.S. Sellar)*

Friday 13 April 1962. This is an unusual photograph in two ways; firstly there is the site which is the little-photographed private platform at Ardeer that served the huge ICI explosives factory there with workmen's trains – these did not appear on the public timetable. Secondly the locomotive is ex-CR Class 812 (LMS Class 3F) 0–6–0 no. 57566 which went on to be preserved. Constructed at St Rollox Works in 1899 she would be withdrawn from service during August 1963 but was purchased by the Scottish Locomotive Preservation Trust. She is currently to be seen working at the Strathspey Railway at Aviemore. *(W.S. Sellar)*

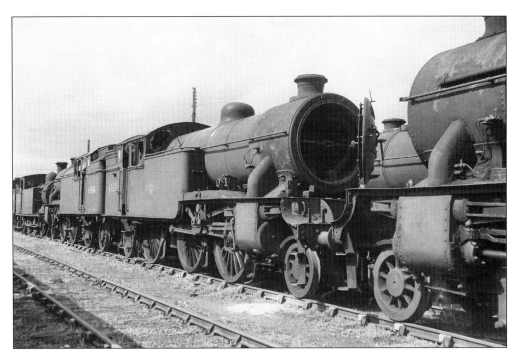

Monday 7 May 1962. This depressing sight is at the Bo'ness dump where many redundant locomotives from the Edinburgh and Glasgow area sheds were sent prior to scrapping. Seen here closest to the camera is ex-LNER Class V3 no. 67625 with, in the background, classmate no. 67650. *(C.J.B. Sanderson/ARPT)*

Thursday 7 June 1962. A relatively rare visitor to Edinburgh is seen here at St Margarets shed; ex-Ministry of Supply WD Class 8F 2–10–0 no. 90774 has probably come into the city with a goods train from Grangemouth, her home shed. Built by the NBL in 1945 for the Ministry of Supply and numbered 73799 by the WD, she at one time bore the name *North British*. Purchased by British Railways during 1948, she would be withdrawn six months after this photograph was taken in December 1962. *(C.J.B. Sanderson/ARPT)*

Friday 27 July 1962. Seen here with a southbound express just after emerging from Penmanshiel tunnel is Class B1 4–6–0 no. 61341 leading ex-LNER Class A3 4–6–2 no. 60088 *Book Law*. The B1 was a product of Gorton Works built during 1948 that would be withdrawn in December 1963, while the A3, named after the 1927 St Leger winner, was constructed at Doncaster Works in 1930 and would be withdrawn just two months prior to the B1 in October 1963. The tunnel, to the north of Grantshouse, suffered a major collapse in March 1979 and was never reopened, a deviation line being constructed. (*C.J.B. Sanderson/ARPT*)

Opposite, top: **Saturday 9 June 1962**. Seen sitting in the yard at Carstairs shed is Carlisle Kingmoor-allocated BR Standard Class 6P5F 'Clan' no. 72008 *Clan Macleod*. (*C.J.B. Sanderson/ARPT*)

Opposite, bottom: **Monday 16 July 1962**. Canonbie station was one of two intermediate stops on the Langholm branch and was opened during April 1864. The platform is looking very clean and tidy as Class 4MT 2–6–0 no. 43139 pauses to pick up passengers. A Doncaster Works-built example of July 1951, she would be withdrawn during September 1967. Passenger services on the branch would only just survive the 100 years to be withdrawn in June 1964 with goods services finishing in September 1967. (*W.S. Sellar*)

Saturday 28 July 1962. Seen here at Eastfield shed in Glasgow, Class B1 4–6–0 no. 61277, bearing a 62B Dundee shed code, has worked into the city earlier in the day and is waiting its next duty. A product of the NBL in 1948 she would be withdrawn during June 1964. *(C.J.B. Sanderson/ARPT)*

Saturday 11 August 1962. First introduced during 1926 to a design by the ex-Lancashire and Yorkshire Railway Chief Engineer, George Hughes, the mixed traffic 2–6–0s that became known as 'Crabs' proved themselves to be powerful and reliable locomotives. Seen here at Hurlford shed is ex-LMS Class 5 no. 42743. Built at Crewe Works in 1927 she would be withdrawn four months after this photograph was taken during December 1962. *(C.J.B. Sanderson/ARPT)*

Thursday 23 August 1962. A busy scene here at Portobello East Junction, looking east, where ex-LNER Class J38 0–6–0 no. 65917, bearing a 65K Polmont shed code, is coming off the Waverley Route with a short train of tar tank wagons. Built at Darlington Works in 1926 she would be withdrawn during November 1966. In the background a two-unit DMU is seen operating a service from Edinburgh to Musselburgh. *(C.J.B. Sanderson/ARPT)*

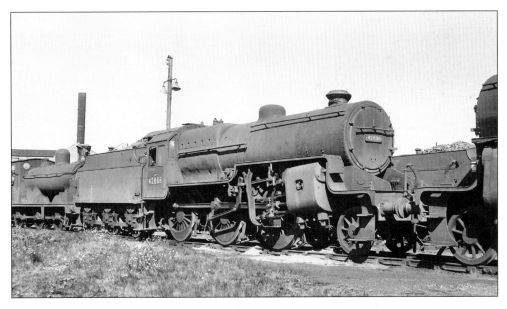

Saturday 8 September 1962. The ex-LMS 'Crab' Moguls were utilised over much of the former LMS territory, in Scotland they found most use working over the old G&SWR area with their last days being spent hauling heavy coal trains in Ayrshire. Seen here at Ayr shed is no. 42808 which was another Crewe Works-built example, entering service in 1929 and being withdrawn three months after this photograph was taken in December 1962. *(C.J.B. Sanderson/ARPT)*

Saturday 8 September 1962. BR Standard Class 4MT 2–6–0 no. 76105 is seen here at Duddingston and Craigmillar station heading westbound with a goods train. She bears a 64C shed code indicating that she was allocated to Dalry Road shed in Edinburgh. Built at Doncaster Works during 1957 she would be delivered new to Kittybrewster shed in Aberdeen and was withdrawn from service only nine years later, in January 1966. *(Author)*

Wednesday 9 January 1963. The severe snowfalls in early January of this year caused delays and cancellations to trains using the Waverley Route between Edinburgh and Carlisle. Seen here in Whitrope cutting with a snow-clearing train is ex-LMS Class 5 4–6–0 no. 45008. One of the early examples of the class constructed at Crewe Works during 1935, she would be withdrawn in May 1964. *(W.S. Sellar)*

Monday 21 January 1963. Waiting to depart from Grangemouth with a passenger train to Larbert is Perth-allocated ex-LMS Class 5 4–6–0 no. 45461. Another Crewe Works member of the class which entered service in 1938, she would be withdrawn during August 1966. *(Author)*

Sunday 17 February 1963. Seen in store at St Margarets shed in Edinburgh is ex-NBR Class G (LNER Class Y9) 0–4–0 saddle tank no. 68095. Built at Cowlairs Works during 1887 she would be the last of this class to be withdrawn from service in December 1962. She had lain at St Margarets for several months awaiting the move into the preservation scene after being purchased privately. She is currently to be seen at the SRPS museum in Bo'ness. *(Author)*

Sunday 17 February 1963. Having technically been withdrawn from service after hauling the 'Pentlands and Tinto Railtour' on 14 October 1961, ex-CR Class 19 (LMS Class 2P) 0–4–4 tank no. 55124 is looking very forlorn at Dalry Road shed in Edinburgh. A veteran of 1895, she would eventually go for scrap during September 1963. *(Author)*

Sunday 17 February 1963. The ex-Caledonian Railway main line between Edinburgh Princes Street and Carstairs traversed the high open moorland around Cobbinshaw and its reservoir and consequently was prone to deep drifting of snow. The locomotive shown here at Dalry Road shed in Edinburgh has just returned from a snow-clearing operation on this line. Ex-LMS Class 5 4–6–0 no. 45367 was constructed by Armstrong Whitworth & Co. in 1937 and withdrawn during November 1963. *(Author)*

Saturday 2 March 1963. Seen here at Prestonpans station, while heading the afternoon Berwick-upon-Tweed slow from Waverley station, is ex-LNER Class A4 4–6–2 no. 60016 *Silver King*. She was constructed at Doncaster Works as the third example of a batch of four locomotives delivered during 1935. They were built specifically to undertake the operation of the 'Silver Jubilee' streamlined service between London and Newcastle which commenced in May 1936. She would be withdrawn from service in March 1965. *(Author)*

Monday 25 March 1963. The cavernous interior of Edinburgh Princes Street station is evident here as ex-LMS Class 5 4–6–0 no. 45361 waits to depart with a train for Carstairs. Another example built by Armstrong Whitworth & Co., this engine entered service during 1937. She was withdrawn in February 1964. Princes Street station was closed during September 1965 with all passenger traffic being transferred to Waverley station. The building would later be demolished and the site turned into a car park. (Author)

Friday 12 April 1963. Seen here at Hawick shed in its final form fitted with a double chimney and smoke deflectors is ex-LNER Class A3 4–6–2 no. 60041 *Salmon Trout*. Compare this photograph with that of the same locomotive on page 43. (C.J.B. Sanderson/ARPT)

Sunday 14 April 1963. Seen here at Duns station is the jointly organised SLS and BLS 'Scottish Rambler No. 2' behind Class B1 4–6–0 no. 61324. The route of the train on this day took in Dunbar, Coldstream, Kelso, Roxburgh, Jedburgh, St Boswells and Hawick. The locomotive was one of the class constructed by the NBL, entering service in 1948 to be withdrawn from service during October 1965. The line between St Boswells and Reston had been opened by the NBR in three stages between 1849 and 1865 to serve the rich agricultural countryside that lay to the south of the Lammermuir Hills. Running mostly through the valley of the Blackadder Water, the line suffered badly in the storms of August 1948 when the section between Greenlaw and Duns was destroyed. Passenger services ceased between St Boswells and Greenlaw but continued on the Duns to Reston section until September 1951. Goods services ceased in July 1965 from St Boswells to Greenlaw and November 1966 from Reston to Duns. *(W.S. Sellar)*

Sunday 28 April 1963. Dwarfed by the fuel storage tanks at Perth shed, BR Standard Class 2MT 2–6–0 no. 78052 sits in the yard. Built at Darlington Works during 1955 she would be allocated new to Motherwell shed only to be withdrawn eleven years later, in January 1966. *(C.J.B. Sanderson/ARPT)*

Wednesday 8 May 1963. A very leaky BR Standard Class 7P6F 'Britannia' 4–6–2 no. 70020 *Mercury* is making slow progress while ascending Borthwick Bank at the head of the 3.25 p.m. Millerhill to Carlisle goods. Built at Crewe Works during 1951 she would be withdrawn in January 1967. *(W.S. Sellar)*

Tuesday 14 May 1963. At the head of the 3.30 p.m. stopper to Berwick-upon-Tweed, ex-LNER Class A3 4–6–2 no. 60043 *Brown Jack* is seen departing Waverley station. By this date she had acquired the distinctive smoke deflectors (see page 95 for an earlier photograph of this locomotive without these deflectors). *(W.S. Sellar)*

Thursday 16 May 1963. The clock atop the North British Hotel shows 10.00 a.m. while below, in the Waverley station in Edinburgh, ex-LMS 'Princess Coronation' Class 4–6–2 no. 46237 *City of Bristol* is preparing to depart at 10.03 a.m. with the service to Perth via Glenfarg. Having arrived in the city earlier on a fill-in turn from Perth, she was scheduled to head back to Crewe, her home shed, later in the day. This locomotive was another of the class to be constructed with streamline casing that would be removed during 1947. *(W.S. Sellar)*

Saturday 18 May 1963. Ex-LMS Class 5 4–6–0 no. 44931, bearing a 63A Perth shed code, moves slowly from Ferryhill shed in Aberdeen and will make its way to the joint station to pick up and work a train south. Constructed at Crewe Works during 1946 she would be withdrawn from service in October 1965. *(Author)*

Saturday 20 July 1963. This portrait photograph of Ivatt-designed Class 2MT 2–6–0 no. 46482 was taken at Dalry Road shed in Edinburgh while the locomotive was apparently being transferred to Ayr shed. She was one of the Darlington Works-constructed examples that appeared after Nationalisation, entering traffic in 1951 and being withdrawn from service in August 1965. *(Author)*

Opposite, top: **Sunday 7 July 1963**. Bearing a 66E Carstairs shed code, ex-LMS Class 5 4–6–0 no. 45245 is seen between duties visiting Dalry Road shed in Edinburgh prior to working back to its home depot. Built by Armstrong Whitworth & Co. in 1936 she would be withdrawn during August 1965. *(Author)*

Opposite, bottom: **Saturday 13 July 1963**. The locomotive shown here stored at Carstairs shed had been withdrawn from service during October of the previous year but was yet to meet the cutter's torch. Ex-CR Class 72 (LMS Class 3P) Pickersgill-designed 4–4–0 no. 54502 had been built by the NBL during 1922 and had worked express passenger trains throughout the old Caley system. One of her last duties, together with classmate no. 54463, had been the haulage of the Glasgow electric 'Blue Train' stock between depots for servicing, both locomotives being fitted with Westinghouse air brake pumps. *(Author)*

Saturday 20 July 1963. An unusual visitor to Dalry Road shed in Edinburgh is BR Standard Class 5MT 4–6–0 no. 73146. Delivered new to St Rollox shed from Derby Works in 1957, this locomotive was fitted with British Caprotti valve gear as this close-up shows. The use of this type of valve gear was promoted for the reasons of economy of maintenance, effectively increasing the locomotive mileage between services. She would be withdrawn only ten years later in May 1967. *(Author)*

Saturday 27 July 1963. With the cylinder drain cocks open, Class 5 4–6–0 no. 44689 accelerates south over Strawfrank water troughs with a train of empty coaching stock. Constructed at Horwich Works during 1950 she would be withdrawn in March 1967. *(Author)*

Opposite: **Wednesday 24 July 1963**. With the long 6.27 p.m. class 'C' goods train behind her, ex-LNER Class A2/3 4–6–2 no. 60522 *Straight Deal* is seen departing from Millerhill Down yard heading for Craiginches. Built at Doncaster Works during 1947 to a design by Edward Thompson and named after the 1943 Derby winner, she would be withdrawn from service in June 1965. *(W.S. Sellar)*

Wednesday 14 August 1963. At the head of the 8.18 a.m. Millerhill to Kingmoor class 'C' goods train, Class A1 4–6–2 no. 60118 *Archibald Sturrock* has paused at Hawick. One of the Doncaster Works-built examples of the class during 1948, she was named after the Scottish-born engineer who became the first Locomotive Superintendent of the Great Northern Railway. She would be withdrawn in October 1965. *(W.S. Sellar)*

Tuesday 27 August 1963. At Tillynaught, the junction for the branch to Banff, BR Standard Class 2 2–6–0 no. 78054 has just arrived from Banff and is preparing to run round its train before the return journey. Constructed at Darlington Works during 1955 and delivered new to Motherwell shed, she would be withdrawn during December 1965 after just a ten-year working life. The branch, which opened in 1859, remained steam-hauled until closure, with passenger services being withdrawn in July 1964 and goods services ceasing during May 1968. *(Author)*

Saturday 14 September 1963. Recovering from a signal check at Eassie on the ex-Caledonian main line between Perth and Aberdeen, ex-LNER Class A3 4–6–2 no. 60090 *Grand Parade* is working the 8.25 a.m. Glasgow Buchanan Street to Aberdeen service. Constructed at Doncaster Works during 1928 and named after the 1919 Derby winner, she would be withdrawn from service in October 1963. *(W.S. Sellar)*

Saturday 28 September 1963. At St Margarets shed in Edinburgh, Class A1 4–6–2 no. 60151 *Midlothian* has been coaled and is waiting to move into the shed. Built in Darlington Works, she entered traffic during 1949 and would be withdrawn in November 1965 having given only sixteen years of service. *(Author)*

Wednesday 25 December 1963. In steam on this Christmas Day at Dalry Road shed in Edinburgh, is ex-NBR Class C (LNER Class J36) 0–6–0 no. 65243 *Maude*. Destined to be withdrawn during July 1966 and go straight into the preservation scene, this locomotive was one of the examples of the class built by Neilson & Co. in 1891 and rebuilt in the form seen here during 1915. She spent time with the R.O.D. in France during the First World War and on her return was named after Lieutenant-General Frederick Stanley Maude. She is currently to be seen at the National Railway Museum in York. *(Author)*

Thursday 27 February 1964. Even during the last few years of main line steam power on British Railways, some sheds still tried hard to keep their locomotives as clean as possible. This ex-LMS Class 5 4–6–0 no. 45053 has been given the treatment by the cleaners at Dalry Road shed in Edinburgh. One of the earlier members of the class, she was built by the Vulcan Foundry in 1934 and would be withdrawn from service in November 1966. *(Author)*

Saturday 21 March 1964. Designed by the LNER's last Chief Mechanical Engineer, A.H. Peppercorn, and constructed at Darlington Works during 1949, Class A1 4–6–2 no. 60152 *Holyrood* was based at Scottish sheds for almost its entire working life except for the last year of service. Seen here bearing a St Margarets shed code, she was to be regularly seen working over the Waverley Route between Edinburgh and Carlisle. She would be withdrawn during June 1965 while based at York shed. None of this class survived into preservation but the A1 Steam Locomotive Trust have built and are currently operating no. 60163 *Tornado* on main line specials. *(Author)*

Friday 27 March 1964. Seen here at Polmadie shed in Glasgow sitting over one of the ashpits is ex-LMS Class 7P 'Royal Scot' no. 46166 *London Rifle Brigade*. Constructed at Derby Works during 1930 she would be rebuilt with a taper boiler in 1945 and was withdrawn from service in September 1964. A long-term resident of Longsight shed in Manchester, by the time of this photograph she was allocated to Carlisle Kingmoor shed. *(Author)*

Friday 27 March 1964. Constructed at Doncaster Works during 1948, Class A2 4–6–2 no. 60535 *Hornet's Beauty* was named after the winner of the 1913 Portland Handicap and she would spend virtually all her working life based at Scottish sheds. Many years at Haymarket and St Margarets in Edinburgh were followed by allocation to Polmadie in Glasgow from where she would be withdrawn in June 1965. She is seen here standing over one of the inspection pits at Polmadie. *(Author)*

Saturday 18 April 1964. Having worked into Aberdeen earlier in the day with a goods train from the south, Class 5 4–6–0 no. 44721 makes a spirited departure from the city with a passenger train heading south past Ferryhill shed. Built at Crewe Works during 1949 she would be withdrawn in August 1965. *(Author)*

Saturday 16 May 1964. Sitting outside Dumfries shed is ex-LMS Class 5 'Crab' 2–6–0 no. 42739 which was built at Crewe Works in 1927. The class consisted of a total of 245 examples built at both Crewe and Horwich Works. This example would be withdrawn during November 1966. *(Author)*

Saturday 23 May 1964. Seen here at Callander station with a full head of steam and looking somewhat overpowered for the work in hand, ex-LNER Class V2 2–6–2 no. 60818 sits at the head of the 11.10 a.m., two-coach Callander to Stirling stopper. Built at Darlington Works in 1937 she would be withdrawn during August 1966. *(W.S. Sellar)*

Tuesday 2 June 1964. The graceful flowing lines of Nigel Gresley's masterpiece class are evident here as ex-LNER Class A4 4–6–2 no. 60004 *William Whitelaw* simmers at St Margarets shed in Edinburgh. Constructed at Doncaster Works during 1937 she would originally be numbered 4462 and named *Great Snipe*, but during 1941 she would be renamed after the LNER's first chairman. One of the last examples of the class to remain in service with British Railways, she was withdrawn in July 1966. *(Author)*

Saturday 20 June 1964. The BR Standard Class of 'Clan' locomotives consisted of only ten examples which were allocated equally between Polmadie shed in Glasgow and Carlisle Kingmoor shed. They were originally destined to work on the Highland line from Perth to Inverness but instead found much useful work on Liverpool and Manchester to Glasgow services and on the difficult 'Port Road' to Stranraer. Seen here is no. 72008 *Clan MacLeod* making a spectacular finish to the 10-mile ascent of Beattock with a six-coach local bound for Glasgow. Constructed at Crewe Works in 1952 she had a short-lived career, being withdrawn during April 1966. None of the class made it into the preservation scene but the Standard Steam Locomotive Company Ltd is currently building the next member of the class numerically, no. 72010 to be named *Hengist. (Author)*

Saturday 4 July 1964. Comrie station had become the terminus for trains from Gleneagles and Crieff after the remainder of the ex-Caledonian scenic line to Lochearnhead and Balquhidder had been closed during October 1951. At this time services were normally undertaken by a four-wheeled railbus, but on this last day of services the powers that be had anticipated a large turnout of passengers for the last train on the branch. Hence, BR Standard Class 4MT 2–6–4 tank no. 80063 of Stirling shed is waiting to depart at 6.45 p.m. at the head of the last train from Comrie. The locomotive was a 1953 product of Brighton Works and would be withdrawn in August 1966. (W.S. Sellar)

Saturday 1 August 1964. With her tender sitting under the coaling plant at Polmadie shed in Glasgow, ex-LMS Class 5 4–6–0 no. 45430 is taking coal prior to moving on to the shed. Constructed by Armstrong Whitworth & Co. during 1937 she would be withdrawn from service in September 1966. (C.J.B. Sanderson/ARPT)

Above: **Sunday 23 August 1964**. With Edinburgh Princes Street station being closed on Sundays, traffic normally arriving there was being transferred to Waverley station. This was accessed by a specially constructed chord between the ex-CR main line at Slateford and the Suburban Circles at Craiglockhart. This day saw BR Standard Class 7P6F 'Britannia' 4–6–2 no. 70013 *Oliver Cromwell* approaching Craiglockhart Junction at the head of the 3.30 p.m. Carstairs to Edinburgh section of an Anglo-Scottish express. The locomotive, built at Crewe Works in 1951, would be central in working the last steam-hauled passenger train run by British Railways, on Sunday 11 August 1968. She has since been restored to main line running and is currently to be seen hauling specials throughout the UK. *(W.S. Sellar)*

Saturday 19 September 1964. Having worked into Crail during the morning, ex-LNER Class B1 4–6–0 no. 61103 is seen here at Cameron Bridge station with the return afternoon working to Thornton Junction that comprised two coaches and a van containing fish. She was another example of the class that was constructed by the NBL. Entering service in 1946, she would be withdrawn in July 1966. *(Author)*

Opposite: **Friday 4 September 1964**. The Waverley station in Edinburgh saw virtually no goods traffic except for the express fish workings from Aberdeen that changed locomotives there. It was therefore unusual to see a westbound ballast train making its way through the station. Class B1 4–6–0 no. 61308 has pounded its way through the Calton Tunnel with its exhaust finally echoing from the rocky face of the Calton Hill as it reached the station approach. This locomotive was a product of the NBL in 1948 and would be withdrawn during November 1966. *(Author)*

Saturday 26 September 1964. The RCTS 'Scottish Lowlander' Railtour was due to traverse the Edinburgh suburban line on this day and a rare photographic opportunity occurred. Having been tipped off that Class A4 no. 60009 *Union of South Africa* was being made available at very late notice for part of the tour, the photographer made his way to Niddrie West Junction to witness the locomotive changeover. The tour had commenced at Crewe with a load of twelve coaches behind no. 46256 *Sir William A. Stanier, F.R.S.* to Carlisle where Class A4 no. 60007 *Sir Nigel Gresley* took over for the run to Niddrie. A Class A3 locomotive was originally detailed for the next section to Glasgow, Kilmarnock, Dumfries and Carlisle but none was available so no. 60009 was substituted and we see her here waiting for the Railtour to arrive at Niddrie. Built at Doncaster Works in 1937, no. 60009 would be withdrawn from service during June 1966 and purchased privately. She has since become a regular performer, hauling specials throughout the UK. *(Author)*

Sunday 4 April 1965. Seen here is another of Nigel Gresley's successes; ex-LNER Class V2 2–6–2 no. 60846 is one example of the 184 members of the class constructed at both Darlington and Doncaster Works between 1936 and 1944. This example came out of Darlington Works during 1939 numbered 4817. Initially allocated to the North Eastern section of the LNER, she was transferred to St Margarets shed during the early 1960s and would be withdrawn in October 1965. *(Author)*

Opposite: **Saturday 31 October 1964**. Seen here at St Margarets shed in Edinburgh in its final form fitted with a double chimney and German-style smoke deflectors is ex-LNER Class A3 4–6–2 no. 60100 *Spearmint*. Constructed at Doncaster Works during 1930 she was named after the 1906 Derby winner and allocated new to Haymarket shed in Edinburgh. She was also based at Aberdeen, Eastfield in Glasgow and Dundee for short periods before joining the St Margarets list in 1963, remaining there until being withdrawn in June 1965. For a period after the Second World War this locomotive was in the hands of a regular Haymarket crew whose driver was the well-known author Norman McKillop. He describes in his book *Enginemen Elite* how much work was involved in bringing the locomotive up to a standard that produced first class performances on the East Coast Main Line for many years. *(Author)*

Monday 26 April 1965. Seen here at Aberdeen station at the head of a train of empty coaching stock, ex-LMS Class 5 4–6–0 no. 44998 is in gleaming condition after an overhaul. She is bearing a 63A Perth shed code and would be spending a few days running in at Ferryhill shed before returning to Perth. One of the 1947 Horwich Works-built examples of the class, she would be withdrawn from service in April 1967. *(Author)*

Saturday 5 June 1965. The two photographs here, taken at St Margarets shed in Edinburgh, show preparations being made for the 'Scottish Locomotive Preservation Fund' special railtour from Waverley to Berwick, Newcastle, Hexham, Carlisle, Hawick and back to Waverley that would be hauled by ex-LNER Class A3 4–6–2 no. 60052 *Prince Palatine*. Constructed at Doncaster Works during 1924 and named after the racehorse of the same name, she is seen here in her final form with double chimney and German-style trough smoke deflectors. This locomotive became the penultimate working example of her class and she would be based at St Margarets during 1963 from where she was to be seen regularly working over the Waverley route. She would be withdrawn from service in January 1966. The diagonal painted yellow stripe on the cabside indicated that she was not permitted to work over lines equipped with overhead electric cables. *(Both photographs Author)*

Above and opposite: **Friday 16 July 1965**. The two photographs on this spread show in some detail ex-LMS Class 5 4–6–0 no. 45477 while at Dalry Road shed in Edinburgh. This was her home as clearly shown by the shed code, 64C, and the name painted on the front buffer beam. She was the product of Derby Works during 1943 and she would be withdrawn in August 1966. Introduced during 1934 to a design by William Stanier, manufacturing of the 'Black 5s' continued in batches for seventeen years until 1951. The 842 members of the class were the product of two independent locomotive builders and three railway works with the first examples coming from the Vulcan Foundry. These were followed over the next four years by locomotives from Armstrong Whitworth & Co. and Crewe Works. From 1943 until 1951 further examples were constructed at Crewe, Horwich and Derby Works. A number of experimental variations were delivered from 1947 onwards; these included locomotives fitted with roller bearings, steel fireboxes and double chimneys. Most striking were the twenty-two examples fitted with Caprotti valve gear, and there was also one locomotive fitted with Stephenson Link Motion which survived into the preservation scene. *(Author)*

Saturday 17 July 1965. Class A2 4–6–2 no. 60532 *Blue Peter* is seen here leaving Dundee Tay Bridge yard with a goods train to Aberdeen. Designed by A.H. Peppercorn and constructed at Doncaster Works during 1948, she was named after the 1939 Derby and 2,000 Guineas winner and allocated initially to York shed. Moved to Haymarket shed in Edinburgh during 1950 she could be seen working express passenger trains on the East Coast Main Line and from 1961 she would be working out of Dundee Tay Bridge shed from where she would be withdrawn on the very last day of 1966. Having been sold privately she was at one time to be seen working on the North Yorkshire Moors Railway and for many years ran main line specials. She is currently on display at the Barrow Hill Roundhouse. *(Author)*

Saturday 17 July 1965. With St Rollox painted on the front buffer beam, BR Standard Class 5MT 4–6–0 no. 73152 is parked in the yard at Dundee Tay Bridge shed. Delivered new to St Rollox shed during 1957 from Derby Works, this locomotive was one of thirty of the class constructed with British Caprotti valve gear, the last ten of which were allocated to St Rollox. The system worked using separate inlet and exhaust poppet valves contained in the cam box mounted on top of the cylinder. The rotary cams were operated by rotating shafts driven from gearboxes attached to the return cranks on the centre driving wheel. This locomotive had an extremely short working life of only eight years before being withdrawn in December 1965. *(Author)*

Saturday 17 July 1965. This veteran locomotive seen at Dundee Tay Bridge shed is ex-NBR Class C (LNER Class J36) 0–6–0 no. 65319. Fitted with a tender cab to give extra protection to crews during adverse weather, she was constructed at Cowlairs Works in 1899 and rebuilt in 1919 in the form we see here. She would be withdrawn during September 1966 having served for sixty-seven years. *(Author)*

Wednesday 24 August 1966. Sitting in bright sunshine in Perth shed yard and looking in comparatively clean condition is ex-LMS Class 5 4–6–0 no. 44997. A product of Horwich Works during 1947 she would be withdrawn in May 1967. *(A.G. Forsyth/Initial Photographics)*

Friday 31 March 1967. This day saw the last steam-hauled goods service from Montrose via Bridge of Dun into Brechin station and the locomotive for the duty has been specially cleaned. Ex-NBR Class S (LNER Class J37) 0–6–0 no. 64611 stands in the yard between movements. This example of the class was constructed by the NBL and entered service during 1920; she would be withdrawn during April 1967. Passenger services into Brechin were withdrawn in August 1952 but goods services carried on for almost another thirty years before being withdrawn in May 1981. The distinctive station at Brechin survived to become part of the Caledonian Railway (Brechin) Ltd which operates the 4-mile branch to Bridge of Dun. *(W.S. Sellar)*